# PEMBROKESHIRE
# FOLK
# TALES

T0347173

# PEMBROKESHIRE
# FOLK TALES

CHRISTINE WILLISON

The
History
Press

*'Some books take you by the hand and lead you into enchanted lands where advice can be ignored at your peril, but if taken can bring you all you have ever wished for. This is one such book. Walk with care and listen intently.'*

John Row, storyteller and poet

First published 2013

The History Press
The Mill, Brimscombe Port
Stroud, Gloucestershire, GL5 2QG
www.thehistorypress.co.uk

Reprinted 2017

British Library Cataloguing in Publication Data.
A catalogue record for this book is available from the British Library.

ISBN 978 0 7524 6565 4

Typesetting and origination by The History Press
Printed in Great Britain by TJ Books Ltd, Padstow, Cornwall

# CONTENTS

# ACKNOWLEDGEMENTS

I wish to thank all my family, particularly my daughters Pippa, Stephanie and Mitzi, who encouraged and believed in me. My grandchildren – Solar, Pixel, Toby and Tiggy – were happy guinea pigs in the early stages of writing. I am grateful to the staff at the archive at St Fagans: Museum of Welsh Life; and to Sue Baldwin, the librarian at Tenby Museum. Support for this book has been worldwide, and I thank Robyn Wright and the children in her class in Melbourne; as well as the teachers and children at Collingwood College, who heard and responded to the early writings. Thanks to my partner for his patience, suggestions, amendments and support, for his help with translations, and particularly for his contribution to the retelling of the stories from the Mabinogion. Thanks also to Lucinda Murray for editing the final manuscript and for her advice throughout. I am grateful to Beth Webb for her foreword, suggestions, and encouragement, and especially for her wise words about chocolate.

# FOREWORD

A good storyteller will say that behind her shoulder stands another storyteller, who heard his tales from a storyteller, who heard … you get the picture.

It sounds a bit daft to say that old stories are old because they are very old, but the point is that some tales just work and even after a thousand years or more, we simply never get sick of them. We might give them a new lick of paint or give the characters new clothes, but the ideas dance on. Tellers with creative flair like Christine Willison have the courage to swap a cart for a clapped-out car if it makes the story more relevant to the listener – but a really good tale timelessly explores the joys, fears and patterns of life that are common to us all – whatever our culture or religion.

The Indigenous Australians have a wonderful tradition of 'Singing up the Land'. This refers to their belief that in ancient times the Ancestors made songs about every detail of the world: rocks, deserts, trees, rivers and even rainbows. As they sang, these things came to be. Where the Ancestors walked, they left their words and music in their footprints. It is these songlines that their descendants now follow as they go walkabout.

As Christine's lovely tales take you on a 'walkabout' across Pembrokeshire, you'll discover that landscape and history are tightly interwoven, often dictating how we think and experience the world. Heaped rocks become wolves in the moonlight, stones have secrets, gold turns to red dust and toads become murderous. Dreams lead to true love and a wild boar keeps a comb and scissors in his bristles!

And each and every tale has its own meaning, tears and laughter. In recent years, the western world has almost lost storytelling and traditional song as a vital part of our culture. Stories old and new offer us awareness of our dreams and hopes; they help us to discover who we are and how we fit into the world.

And this is something Christine is particularly good at.

I first met her one particularly wet Glastonbury Festival. She was organising the storytelling in the Earth Lodge on the Green Field. It was my first booking as a teller at such a big event and I was rather scared and lost. She took me into her caravan, fed me, gave me bottled water from her own Pembrokeshire springs and told me stories – wonderful, magical, spellbinding tales, some of which she has recorded here.

'Always remember,' she said, 'when you are telling a story, take your time, sit back, smile and let the listener wait, for you have something they don't … the ending.'

So allow me to invite you into Christine's world of Pembrokeshire folk tales. Pour yourself some spring water, treat yourself to a piece of homemade cake and listen.

As some old tellers like to say: 'Make yourselves comfy and we'll put food in the eating place, drink in the drinking place and stories in the listening place.'

*Croeso!*

*Beth Webb* (www.bethwebb.co.uk)

# INTRODUCTION

I have collected these tales from my existing repertoire and original research. Firstly I made a list of towns and villages to have broad geographic coverage. I then toured the county looking, noting, and taking photos. I researched in museum and library archives. I uncovered many tales and innumerable anecdotes. Two tales are from the Mabinogion. Many parts of Wales lay claim to these stories, but Pembrokeshire or Dyfed (the ancient name for south-west Wales) are specifically mentioned in the stories retold here, and support the claim that this western county is the true home of the ancient legends.

Some spellings, particularly of place names, have many different versions. Both languages of Wales have grown and changed, and are subject to translation and misunderstanding. This can create confusion for readers, but also adds colour and flavour. I have included different spellings as they appeared in original papers and archives. I have retained some archaic phraseology from Lady Charlotte Guest's translation of the Mabinogion, whilst attempting to remove some of the Victorian overtones. I hope it gives you a feel for the ancient times in which the stories were first told.

I have, as all storytellers do, taken a few liberties with names and settings. None of the essence of the stories, or the places in which they are purported to have taken place, have changed. It is rather like the story I was once told about a traditional African village where each of the houses had changed only by the addition of a television aerial. My friend asked why people still assembled at the end of the day at the storyteller's house, because surely the stories on television were just as good. The respondent informed my friend that the stories were better because the storyteller knew them.

Much of this tour through the tales and traditions of Wales' far-west is a journey through countryside. The English word countryside is revealing: it sees the rural world standing to one side of the hectic urban mainstream. The Welsh equivalent is quite different – *cefn gwlad* – literally, the country's backbone, the core from which the whole land takes strength. The Preseli Hills, at the centre of Pembrokeshire, are very much the county's backbone; and the tales that arise from the very rocks and cliffs of this place are as ancient and resistant as the landscape.

*Christine Willison, 2013* (www.christinestories.co.uk)

# PRONUNCIATION GUIDE

## WELSH CONSONANTS

As in English with the following exceptions:

| | |
|---|---|
| c | carol – never as in cedar |
| ch | loch – never as in churlish |
| dd | this – never as in think |
| f | of – never fat |
| ff | off – never of |
| g | girl – never gem |
| ng | sing – never angel |
| h | hat – never silent |
| ll | put your tongue in the 'l' position then breathe out |
| r | trilled or rolled as in Italian |
| rh | put your tongue in the 'r' position then blow |
| s | sit – never rose |
| si | when followed by a vowel (siop) pronounced sh as in shop |
| th | thin – never the |

## WELSH VOWELS

Can be short or long:

| | | |
|---|---|---|
| a | hanes/cat | ar/father |
| e | cerdyn/pet | cewch/bear |

| i | chwilio/sit | i/machine | |
|---|---|---|---|
| o | os/pot | to/more | |
| w | dwfn/cook | cwn/pool | |
| y | Crymych/sit | ty/machine | yna/cut |

## Dipthongs

| ae, ai, au | aye |
|---|---|
| aw | ah + oo |
| ei, eu, ey | ay |
| iw, uw | dew |
| oe, oi | oil |
| ow | Owen – not down |
| yw | ee + oo |
| wy | gooy – two vowels compressed into one syllable |

## Pronunciation of some common names

| Cai | Kigh |
|---|---|
| Culhwch | Kil – hooch (with a guttural ch) |
| Owain | Oh wine |
| Pwyll | Pooy – ll |
| Rhiannon | Hree – an – on |
| Ysbaddaden | Us – bath – ad – en |

Pembrokeshire
Sir Benfro

Pen Cemaes

Poppit
Llandudoch
St Dogmaels

Pen Dinas

Trewyddel
Moylgrove

Aberoyel

Pen caer

Nanhyfer
Nevern

Cwm Cych

Llanwnda

Wdig
Goodwick
Abergwaun
Fishguard
Cwm Gwaun

Dinas

Trefdraeth
Newport

Peatcelfan

Brynberian

Crymych

Abercastle
Trefin

Mynydd Preseli

Maenclochog

Ramsey

Wolf's Castle

Tyddewi
St David's
Solfach
Solfa

Roch

Druidstone

Haverfordwest
Hwlffordd

Narberth
Arberth

Hangrove
beaty

Broadhaven

Skomer

Skokholm

Milford
Haven

Neyland

Redberth

Saundersfoot

Pembroke Dock

Pembroke
Penfro

Manorbier

Tenby

Orielzon

Castlemartin

Caldey

St Govan's Head

# Pembrokeshire Folk Tales

## The Long House

The journey begins at home.

April. I am sitting in my studio, once a barn for cows. If I think hard I can imagine them chewing the cud, being hand-milked and lowing gently. The problem is that too many thoughts and demands encroach on my writing time. If it isn't the flower border, it's the vegetable garden, with hedge-banks to shelter it from the wind, sticks to prop up peas and beans, and Brussels sprouts neatly stripped by caterpillars and slugs. We must have the best-fed slugs in the county, produce grown naturally, without chemicals. A perfect feed.

The truth is my thoughts wander too readily because I am a bit stuck. I have done my research, adapted some of my repertoire of oral stories and met people to hear their anecdotes. Perhaps I'll go and do some baking for inspiration.

My home is an ancient, traditional Pembrokeshire long house. Very typically the original *bwthyn*, or hovel, had three rooms, one of which was a kitchen, which is the height of two rooms – this helped the house keep cool in summer and enabled things to be hung in the rafters. It is the main room of the house and serves as a place to cook and eat – everything necessary for the running of a home and for relaxing, although I suspect there was little of that in the old days.

The second ground-floor room, off the kitchen, now a sitting room, was a bedroom with its open fire and smoke-blackened chimney, where probably, the farmer, his wife and various elderly relatives slept. Above this room, reached via a ladder from the kitchen, is a *Croglofft* – a room right under the eaves, where grain was stored and children slept (out of the way of rats).

As the farm prospered and grew, and as livestock became more plentiful, a barn was added to the north-east end of the house, then another, used as a cow byre. As time went on, further barns were added. Eventually, the original barn next to the house was turned into a dairy, where butter and cheeses were made.

Finally, 200 or so years ago another barn was added as a cart house, together with two calf pens. The roofline reflects the additions over the centuries by being higgledy-piggledy. All barns can be accessed from the kitchen. Farm workers in past times slept in *Croglofft* areas above the various barns. It was primitive but I am sure very cosy. It was a firmly held belief that cows who saw the light from the fire gave better milk.

There has been a settlement on this site for centuries, always constructed from the rocks and stones lying on the land and sometimes just beneath the surface. On occasion now, in the twenty-first century, we curse these very stones for distorting or breaking the blades of mowing machines. Perhaps they have always borne the brunt of bad temper in the growing season. But their very density and robust quality is what has made them useful as building materials.

But it isn't of course just about the stone. Settlements were always built close to a good and reliable water supply, my reason too for wishing to live in the house which exists today: delicious sweet water unadulterated by chemical additives and always on tap. We drink it, bathe in it, water our plants and vegetables with it and couldn't feel more indulged.

The stones from which the walls of the house are constructed are similar to the neighbouring bluestones that were taken (somehow – and that's another story) to Stonehenge, for building that megalith.

These stones have memories imprinted in their heart and on their surface. Sights and sounds now fleetingly glimpsed and heard in the whispers and sighs and creaks that all old buildings make. It is a colourful backdrop and an inspiration for the creation of oral and written stories which I love to share with people of all ages, hopefully inspiring my listeners and readers to create their own tales.

Some time ago I was invited to a quiet corner in the north part of this beautiful, magical county, to find out more about *Plant Rhys Dwfn* – the little people – sometimes called the *Tylwyth Teg*, mischievous fairies who reputedly enjoy teasing, but sometimes provide help when it is needed and who play a large part in the stories of this place.

# LLANDUDOCH, ST DOGMAEL'S

The elderly woman had many stories to share and much information about Llandudoch – St Dogmael's, where she lived. Because she spoke only Welsh, I took my partner, a Welsh speaker, along with me to translate:

> There was a man in St Dogmael's who was one hundred years old when he died. Revered as a wise man, he used to say that the whole neighbourhood was considered 'fou' (a place of fairies.) It was, apparently, a common experience for men to be led astray all night. After marvellous adventures and frightening excursions,

which seemed as if they would be endless, they found that when day broke, they were close to their own homes.

One man, who was led astray on his way home from a day working with the blacksmith, happened to have with him a number of hoop rods. (Hoop rods are what the blacksmith uses to make hoops. The rods are heated in the forge and hammered into shape ready for the cooper to use in making barrels). As he was transported about by the spirits he dropped the rods one at a time. The next day he gathered together his friends and neighbours to follow the dropped rods and retrace his footsteps. They were surprised to find that the rods were scattered over many miles of countryside.

Another time, a St Dogmael's fisherman was returning home from a wedding at Moylgrove. It was very dark and he had been celebrating. The fairies led him astray, but after a few hours and a bit of sobering up he spotted the North Star in the sky and used it to navigate his way home.

On another occasion the mischievous faeries forced an elderly and 'not so sprightly' clerical person to join in the magic dance of 'St Dogmell's' and kept him dancing there until morning. The poor man spent several days in bed recovering from exhaustion following this adventure.

This was the work of the *ellyllon* (elves) who led all these folk astray, and put a 'cap of oblivion' on their heads, which prevented them from ever telling their adventures clearly.

Her words drew me into a world about which I had only previously read. She continued:

There are many stories which describe how easy it is for a mortal to enter the 'Otherworld' through fairy circles. For centuries there have been reports of fairies dancing, their little feet making a ring on the ground. If they discover that they are being observed they like nothing better than to persuade the observer to join them. Some people have run away, and then regret not being brave enough to join the fairies in their dance. Some have reported good to come from this, and others have reported evil.

The old woman paused, stared at me intently, leaned forward, and spoke in a way that left me in no doubt that she was serious:

There are three places in this county from where you can either see the Otherworld, or start a journey to it. The first is Pen Cemaes (Cemaes Head at the mouth of the River Teifi), where it is possible to see the land of *Plant Rhys Dwfn* sometimes called *Tylwyth Teg* or fairy folk. At Pen Cemaes you must stand on exactly the right spot to see this land. Unfortunately, no one can tell you where that is.

I had heard many stories about this magical place, now I leaned forward making it difficult for my partner to hear her soft words. There was more:

Arberth (Narberth), the second place, is named in the Mabinogion as the place where Pwyll, Prince of Dyfed first met Rhiannon, who was to become his wife. There is a mound just on the edge of the town, where you will find the ruins of Narberth Castle. If you are brave enough, you can sit on the mound, just as Pwyll did over six hundred years ago. You may either see a wonder beyond your wildest imaginings or be dealt severe and wounding blows. It is also said that this mound is an entrance to the Otherworld.

Cwm Cych is the third place she told me about:

This is a place of turmoil. Here the entrance to the Otherworld is easy to find, but impossible to pass through, unless you are favoured. Indeed it is a memorable place, and at this very spot the three counties of Pembrokeshire, Ceredigion and Carmarthenshire meet.

These fascinating pieces of information, translated for me by my partner, whetted my appetite. When I reached home my head was filled with the old woman's advice and snippets of stories were whirling around in my head. I made notes about the places, marked them on a map, and decided that I would see them at first hand to embed the images in my mind, and add colour to the many stories. Sunny weather several days later cemented my resolve to find out for myself. So I packed a rucksack, put on my walking boots and headed for Pen Cemaes, the first place mentioned by the woman.

# POPPIT SANDS

I decided to start at Poppit Sands, from where Pen Cemaes can be viewed. I have been told that the name Poppit is derived from 'Pot Pit' and that the clay in that place was coveted by local potters. As I sat on the sand dunes, looking out to sea, I remembered the story of Dai Pots, a potter from Cardigan on the other side of the River Teifi. Dai had a secret spot amongst these very sand dunes, where he dug the clay from which he threw beautiful earthenware. He then fired them in a Heath Robinson-style wood-fired kiln. Alas, Dai Pots was lost in a boating accident on a Scottish loch. The accident mystified his friends because Dai was well-known locally as a competent swimmer and boatman. This was many years ago, but at home we still have some of his beautiful jugs made from Poppit clay.

Walking along the beach to get a better view of Pen Cemaes, I came across a cleverly constructed castle, with flags and a castellated wall which surrounded four central towers. A wooden fence provided an avenue towards the main entrance of the castle. Building it had taken time, care and attention to detail. I smiled at the thought that this castle would be washed away with the morning tide. Strange how as an adult this becomes poetry, but a child would be saddened by the loss of their creation.

Realising that I needed to get closer, I walked along the lane that winds towards Pen Cemaes. As I approached it, the peninsula looked like a goat swimming in the sea.

I thought how powerful the elements were, how even though we imagine that we are sophisticated, the wind, the sea, the earth and the sun still control our actions.

Upon reaching the headland, I climbed over a stile into what is now a nature reserve. It was a sunny day in spring, and birds were actively swooping and diving into the yellow-flowered gorse, the clumps of heather and the reeds. I listened to the sounds they made; in my reverie I stood at the cliff edge and looked out to sea. I was taken aback when I saw an island shrouded in mist. Upon checking the map, there was no island shown. Perhaps it was a ship, come too close to the rocks. Then the wind became strong and blew away the mist. There was neither island nor ship. It was probably a trick of the light, sparked off by my imagination.

As I sat on a mound to study the map, a hedgehog came past. He stopped, lifted his head and looked at me, went along a well-worn path, stopped, looked over his shoulder, shuffled further, and then looked over his shoulder again. Usually when this creature senses danger, it curls into a ball to protect itself from predators. But this animal was behaving oddly. Clearly it wanted me to follow. It reminded me of a story about a shepherd who was from here.

## The Shepherd of Allt y Goed

Once, long ago, in a place not far from Pen Cemaes, there lived a shepherd, Dewi Rhys. He barely scratched a living from tending his sheep. After paying for the grazing in the nearby woodland, there was barely enough left from the sales of wool and animals at the end of the season to keep him, his wife and baby daughter.

But he was deliriously happy. He loved his wife and baby very much. He was content that he could provide for them. They lived in a tiny cottage, just one room up and one down. Upstairs, where they slept, was reached by a ladder, and had a bed with a straw mattress. Downstairs, the room was sparsely furnished with bits and pieces from relatives.

On the day of our story, Dewi woke as soon as he heard the cockerel crowing in the nearby farmyard. That morning he wanted to set off early because the day before he had noticed one of his ewes looking uncomfortable. Her first lamb was due any day and he wanted to be with her in case she needed help.

He got out of bed quietly, so as not to disturb his wife and daughter, went down the ladder, and lit the fire in the range so that it would be warm for his family when they arose. In the yard outside he washed in icy cold water from the pump. That certainly washed the sleep from his eyes. Dewi Rhys rubbed himself dry with a towel hanging on the range and warmed himself by the fire. He put on the clothes which he had left on the fireside chair the night before. At the table he cut himself two nice doorsteps of bread – not those nice dainty slices that his aunts cut for Sunday tea.

These thick slices would sustain him for the day. He spread them both with dripping from the pot, put them together, wrapped them in a clean cloth and put them in his bag along with a bottle of water. He stoked the fire in the range and went upstairs to kiss his wife and daughter who were just waking and had that sleepy look which he adored. He gently tweaked his daughter's cheek, which made her giggle. He waved from the top of the steps, went down the ladder, and then went out of the cottage and along the garden path. At the gate he looked back and smiled, and as he did so the door opened and his wife and baby waved to him, framed by the open door of the cottage. He blew a kiss and went on his way. He smiled as he went and counted his blessings.

He was in such a dream that he almost tripped over the *draenog* which was sitting in the middle of the path. He looked at the creature; it looked back at him and blinked. Dewi Rhys was surprised; usually these small creatures rolled into a ball when they sensed danger, using their prickly spines as a defence. But this animal looked at him with its bright round eyes, turned and walked away from him, then looked over its shoulder and looked at him, then shuffled along the path again and looked over its shoulder again. It was as if the hedgehog wanted him to follow.

He decided to leave the ewe to fend for herself. This was an adventure! He followed the *draenog*. It led him past the place in the forest where his sheep were grazing, further into the deepest, darkest part of the woodland, rarely visited by woodland dwellers. The creature made its way to a large stone which blocked the pathway. It pushed at the stone with its sharp, pointed nose and looked at him. It seemed to Dewi Rhys that the *draenog* wanted him to move the obstacle. Dewi pushed it, but it was heavy. He tried again and eventually it shifted. He shoved again and it moved some more, to reveal the edge of something shiny underneath. Our shepherd's eyes widened and he put all his effort into moving the stone.

Underneath was a gold coin! Never in his life had he seen a gold coin before. He picked it up. This was more money than he could have ever imagined. He turned it over, and over again. It really was a gold coin. He put it in his pocket and looked around to see if anyone was watching. By now the *draenog* had disappeared. Dewi ran and ran all the way home.

His wife was surprised to see him return. Last night he had told her about having to be up early to look after the ewe, and now here he was back at home. She was concerned, was something wrong? She started to question him but he pushed past her with a strange look on his face, went up to their bedroom and reached underneath the mattress for the small wooden box he kept there.

Somebody had once given him this box for treasures. He opened the box, it was empty – no treasures were secreted there. He carefully placed the gold coin inside the box, and looked round to see if he had been observed. He was alone in the room. He placed the box back under that mattress and went down the ladder to the room below. His wife continued questioning him, noticing he still had that strange look on his face. He ignored her questions, left the house and went to tend his sheep.

He sat by his sheep that day dreaming about the coin and what it could buy. Maybe he could buy his wife a dress. She hadn't had a new dress since her mother had made her wedding dress. Perhaps she would prefer a new bonnet, or maybe they should buy something for the baby. On the other hand, it was probably enough to buy his own piece of land. Then he could graze the sheep on his own land and avoid payments to landowners. His thoughts took him through the day. He barely paid any attention to his sheep and almost forgot to eat his bread and dripping.

When he arrived home, he was greeted by the warm smells of cooking and the dimpled smiles of his daughter. His wife looked troubled. She asked him again what had happened this morning. Why had he returned? Why was he rummaging around in the upstairs room? He told her she didn't need to trouble herself. She was insistent, but he wanted to keep the news of the find to himself, so he determined not to tell her, no matter how many times she asked. There was, for the first time ever in their marriage, a frosty silence over supper.

Next morning he didn't dally in bed, no extra hug for his wife, and he rose as soon as he heard the cockerel crow. Getting ready quickly, Dewi Rhys didn't think he had time to light the fire, and didn't kiss his wife and baby before he left. He wanted to check that place again. He ran through the forest until he reached the stone. Someone had put it back to its original position. He pushed it to one side again, to reveal – another gold coin!

His eyes gleamed as he saw it. He bent down and picked it up, put it in his pocket, looked round to see if anyone had seen, and then ran home. His wife was shocked at his early return, but when she started to question him again, he pushed her to one side and climbed the ladder to the upstairs room. He reached under the straw mattress, pulled out the box, opened the lid and put the second coin in with the first. He closed the lid and pushed the box back under the mattress, and then made his way downstairs.

His wife started to question him again but he left quickly to avoid another argument. He wanted to keep the coins a secret. After all, he told himself, it would be a nice surprise for his wife if this continued and they became rich landowners. He also worried that someone else would hear about his good fortune and perhaps try to steal his coins.

That evening when he returned home, he and his wife sat at the table and ate supper in silence. She was concerned that something was going on. He had changed, he hardly noticed her or their daughter. He had an odd look on his face, was inattentive, didn't answer her questions, and appeared not to hear anything she said.

After the meal was finished, there was not the usual warm thanks from her husband: he didn't help to clear away the dishes and he didn't pick up their daughter for her usual goodnight *cwtch* (cuddle).

After putting the child to bed, his wife tried again to find out what was going on. She stood at the end of the table and spoke. She raised her voice and finally shouted to get his attention. He looked up in surprise. She then asked what was going on. He was annoyed. Nothing was going on, he said. What did she mean? She explained her fears, but instead of telling her about his good fortune, he kept it to himself. He said it was none of her business.

This infuriated her. 'We are partners,' she said. 'We promised to share everything and to tell each other everything. There is something you are not telling me and I am concerned!'

He told her to stop badgering him; he was tired and going to bed.

That night they slept as far away from each other as the bed would allow; she on one edge of the mattress and he on the other, with their backs to each other and with a cold panel down the middle of the bed – and no touching.

The next morning he got up and she followed him to the downstairs room. Her eyes were red and swollen with crying and with insufficient sleep. She insisted on having the truth of it. He was determined that she would not. Again she reminded him about their marriage, their partnership – their promises.

He became angry and shouted at her. She cried, and when she cried the baby cried, as they always do. Dewi Rhys left the house saying that he needed to get away from the noise. No wash under the pump, no fire lit, and no hugs and kisses for his wife and baby. No bottle of water, no bread and dripping. But he was determined, and he was late.

He ran down the garden path; she didn't even expect him to turn and wave as he used to. He ran along the lane, through the forest, and then froze. There, on the path in front of him, was another figure, making his way in the same direction, through the forest.

It was Harri Pritchard, the miller's son. Dewi Rhys needed to get in front of him, so he started to run. Harri looked round and he started to run too. Dewi speeded up; so did Harri. They both ran through the forest, but the miller's son reached the stone first. He pushed it to one side with ease. He was a muscular man who spent his working life moving sacks of grain and sacks of flour, moving and fitting millstones and milling grain. He reached down and picked up the glittering gold coin. He had a gleam in his eye as he pocketed the coin.

Dewi reached the stone, panting and breathless. He looked at Harri and put out his hand. 'Give it to me, it's mine!'

'No it's not,' said Harri. 'Finder's Keeper's – I found it, I'm keeping it.'

'But it's mine, I was led to this place, it's rightfully mine!'

'No it's not!'

Dewi pushed the flattened palm of his hand closer to Harri. 'Give it to me, it's mine!'

'No!'

'Yes!'

The argument went on for some time, the two men starting to shout at each other. Their eyes blazed as they looked at each other.

Both were set on having the gold coin. Once, these two men had been friends, but now they eyed each other with contempt, each sure of his rights.

Then Dewi Rhys, that gentle shepherd, did something contrary to his usual gentle nature. He made his hand into a fist and punched Harri Pritchard on the nose.

Harri Pritchard was surprised and insulted, but not hurt. That puny shepherd could not hurt him. But he had had enough of the annoying Dewi Rhys. He now made his hand into an extremely large fist, and punched Dewi on the nose. He knocked him out cold and left him there, with blood trickling from his nose, to cool off.

When Dewi recovered consciousness, he rubbed his sore nose, frowned, stood up, brushed himself off, and then made his way to the field where his sheep were grazing. He sat, scowling all day. No food, no drink, a sore nose and, what was worse, no gold coin!

That night when he went home his wife saw his injured nose and approached him with sympathetic words, but he was having none of it. They ate in silence and both retired to bed. Once again they slept as far away from each other as the bed would allow, she on one edge of the mattress and he on the other, with their backs to each other and with a cold panel down the middle of the bed and no touching.

Next morning he got up when it was still dark, before the cockerel crowed and while the moon still shone brightly. He had hardly slept, angry at the loss of the coin, angry at his wife's behaviour, angry that the baby, sensing the tension in the house, had kept him awake with her crying. He went into the downstairs room, dressed, and went straight out of the door, no wash at the pump, for the second day. He knew that he smelled bad, but had no time. No bread and dripping, no drink, no fire lit, but he was making sure he would get there first.

He ran and ran until he reached the stone. The first light of dawn was barely showing. He pushed the stone to one side in haste and what seemed like anger. There, under the stone was … well it was flat and disc-shaped, definitely the shape of a coin, but it was just red dust! He let out a yell, and kicked at the stone, which hurt his toe. He stamped and stamped on the ground, which hurt the soles of his feet. He felt close to tears. Then he stopped, a look of horror came over his face. This small, flat disc-shaped pile of red dust had clearly once been a coin. His face went white as a thought struck him: what about the coins at home?

He ran and ran until he got home, and rushed straight up the ladder to the room upstairs. His wife said nothing – she had become used to her husband behaving oddly and badly. She stood in the downstairs room and tapped her foot. The baby started crying.

Dewi Rhys reached under the straw mattress and drew out the box. Very carefully he prised open the lid. Then he let out a loud yell as if he had been injured.

His wife, thinking that he had been hurt, raced up the ladder. She saw her husband on his knees beside the bed with his head in his hands, crying.

She knelt beside him and stroked the back of his neck. 'Oh, dear,' she said, 'I knew that there must be something wrong, you've been behaving so oddly of late, tell me, what is it?'

Dewi Rhys wailed and snivelled for a while, then haltingly told her the story of the *draenog*, the stone, the gold, the box, the fight with Harri, the red dust. 'And I wanted it to be a surprise for you; I didn't want you to worry.'

She stiffened as she listened to the story, her eyes widening. When he finished telling her the story, she stood up and looked at him in disbelief.

'You fool!' she said.

'What do you mean?' he said. 'I did it for us, so that we could have our own land. We would have been rich!'

'But instead, you have put us all in great danger.' Her eyes were blazing.

'How have I done that?'

'We didn't need riches, we have always managed and we have always been happy, we had each other and we have our daughter. You have jeopardised all of that with your greed!'

'How?'

'You should know, but I remember now how you were as a boy. You didn't listen to your grandmother's stories, nor those of you mother. They tried to pass their wisdom on to you but you always knew better!'

'How do the old wives' tales help us?'

'Listen to me and don't interrupt.' She had never sounded so fierce before. 'You have put us, and particularly our child, in danger. If you had only listened to your mother and your grandmother you would know that the *draenog* is a common disguise used by the *Tylwyth Teg*. They like nothing better than to make their way into a house where there is a baby, and frequently use magic red dust to gain entry. Then they steal the baby and replace it with one of their own. You have brought the evil red dust into our home and placed our child in danger!'

Dewi Rhys' face turned ashen. His eyes darted over to the child sleeping peacefully. 'What can I do to make amends?'

'Take the box away, and take great care not to spill the red dust. Then out in the yard, set fire to it, burn it and its evil contents. Take off your clothes. Wash yourself at the pump, put on clean clothes. Only then can you return to the house.'

Dewi Rhys took the box, carried it and its contents into the yard behind the house and placed it on a pile of dry twigs, leaves and weeds, and lit a fire. He placed the box on top and waited until it and its dangerous contents were completely reduced to ashes. All that remained were the two brass hinges that held the box and its lid together, blackened in the ashes of the fire. He buried the two hinges under the chicken house. Then he went to the pump, and not before time, took off all his clothes and scrubbed himself clean in the cold water. She brought him a towel and fresh clothes. She watched as he took the dirty clothes to the fire and burnt them as well. Having rubbed himself dry and put on clean clothes, he then returned to the house. He picked up the baby, kissed her and watched her face dimple into smiles. She had missed her father and his gentle ways.

His wife came into the house carrying a bunch of herbs, sage, rosemary, thyme and a sprig from the cedar tree. She bound the bunch tightly with twine, went to the fire in the range, opened the fire box, lit the herbs, and then blew out the flames. She then took the feather of a buzzard and fanned the smoke into every corner of the house. Dewi was instructed to close the windows and doors, close the shutters and lock them securely. His wife fanned the smoke around the windows and doorways, until she was sure that their home was fully protected, just as her mother and grandmother had instructed her.

All that day the shepherd and his wife stayed inside the house. They cleaned and they cooked, never letting the child out of their sight. That evening they both sat by the bed as she slept, not daring to leave her. They sat there all evening and into the night.

At midnight, had they been brave enough to peep from one of the shutters, they would have seen the *draenog* making its way up the lane, then along the garden path until it reached their door. They might, if they had peeped, have seen the creature push at the door with its sharp pointed nose. The animal made three circuits of the house, trying a window here and a mouse hole there, but failed to gain entry. If they had been brave enough to look they would have seen the hedgehog return up the garden path, pause at the gate, and stand up on its hind legs. Then they would have seen those hind legs grow longer, the forelegs become arms. The sharp pointed snout disappear, the head become round and the spines become hairs. The *draenog* became a short, plump, hairy man who jumped into the air, clicked his heels together and disappeared.

But they saw none of this. They only heard rustling, shuffling and snuffling outside. They were terrified and didn't dare move; hardly dared breathe. They both stayed awake all night. In the morning the wife opened the doors, the windows and the shutters, walked cautiously around the house and then declared that it was safe.

Dewi Rhys breathed a sigh of relief, washed at the pump, lit the fire, made his wife a cup of tea and encouraged her to sleep while he spent the day looking after his beautiful daughter. He cooked supper for them all and then woke his wife. He asked her to forgive him. She did, but on one condition: that he would ask his mother

and grandmother to teach him all their stories so that he could then tell them to his children. He readily agreed.

Now he understood that his real riches were his wife and daughter. He never wished for gold again. He and his wife fell in love a second time and their love continued into old age. They had many more children, who loved to hear stories, and who passed them on to their own children. You could say that they all lived happily ever after.

If you come to this part of Wales, you might just meet their descendants – and they might tell you a story.

I came out of my reverie and remembered where I was. I seemed to be re-enacting the story of Dewi Rhys. With some trepidation and a distinct feeling of déjà vu, I stood up and walked along the path, following the small creature. We walked and walked until we came to a large stone on the path in front of us. This was uncanny. My feet curled with anxiety. The hedgehog pushed at the stone with his nose, then looked up at me, then pushed again at the stone, then looked up at me. I felt chilled: this was a bit too familiar. What was I doing here? Was I already in danger?

But I couldn't walk away. I was hooked into a story and needed to see it through.

Evidently the hedgehog wanted me to move the stone. It was as high as my shoulder and looked exceedingly heavy. I pushed and pushed, put my shoulder to the stone and heaved and pushed. Eventually the stone moved a little, and then swung to one side to reveal a small hole in the ground, and what seemed to be stone steps spiralling down into the earth below. But I couldn't be sure, because the hole was small and deep and dark. The hedgehog went into the hole, I didn't see it again. Even if the hole had been big enough for me to go in, I didn't feel brave enough.

The wind blew and it started to rain. I decided to go home and write some more stories. On the way back I met a young man, the new owner of the farm at Allt y Goed. He was renovating the farm and installing new buildings to give campers modern facilities. He mentioned that he had felt an urge last year to keep sheep on the land, but had been too kind-hearted to send the lambs to market to be slaughtered, particularly as he had given them all names. This year he was having to content himself with selling only the fleeces.

As I continued my journey I smiled thinking how Dewi Rhys would have been helpful here.

Two or three days later, the sun was shining and I felt drawn to pursue the *draenog*. I told myself that it was just to complete some sketches for this book. I made for the place where I had seen the *draenog* disappear into the hole in the ground. The stone had been replaced. I pushed and struggled to move it. Some walkers came by, looking at me oddly. I realised that a lone woman pushing at a standing stone was a strange sight. I sat on a nearby hump. The wind blew something in my eye, so I searched in my rucksack and found a small mirror, cleaned the grit from my eye and bathed it with drinking water in the cap from my water bottle.

When my eye stopped streaming, I blinked. There was a small person standing next to the stone. He looked perturbed and was obviously searching for something.

I have a fiercely independent friend of small stature who will never ask for help, even when something has been inconsiderately placed out of reach. She would rather go without. So as I felt I should at least show willing. I approached and asked the man if he needed a hand. He looked at me, then took a deep breath, and said that he was looking for a key. I asked if I could help. He nodded. We scoured the land around the stone. When I asked him what sort of key we were looking for, he gave me a funny look. Perhaps he could describe the key. He did his best and indicated, with his fingers, the size of the key – it was quite large. It didn't help, we still couldn't find it.

He started to look very miserable and explained that the key was one of several tokens that he must find in order to return home. It seemed that he was lost here, and the way home was to be found only on production of many items. At the top of the list were three silvery-green hairs from a mermaid's hairbrush. He continued to mutter about a key, a ring, and a box. These were all familiar items to me. They have been appearing in stories for centuries. In fact I have a collection of similar objects which I take to story making workshops to use as visual prompts for stories.

I was intrigued, but stopped to think. This was more than just lending a hand to someone in need, it sounded like a huge task – I couldn't just dive in. I started to explain that I could help today but I would be in trouble with my publisher if I missed their deadline. He looked mystified and miserable, and I started to feel guilty. How much time could it possibly take to find a few things? Then it was my turn to be mystified. What was the importance of the objects? How would they help him? Why these particular items? Where was he from? How would he get back? I had many questions, but he put up his hand.

'You offered help, are you now taking away the offer? I can't explain any of the things you ask. But I will make a bargain with you. If you agree to help I will give you a story at every place we visit.'

It was tempting. I had become a bit stuck and my research was taking ages, so perhaps the time would be well spent after all. I tried to question him again, but he clamped his jaws shut in a way that reminded me of my mother when I was a teenager. Despite his bad demeanour and poor manners, I still felt drawn towards the quest for objects, though not to him. I took another deep breath, and agreed to help him. He almost smiled.

I suggested that we should meet the next day at Llandudoch (St Dogmael's), to follow up the legend of a mermaid being seen there. It seemed as good a starting place as any. My new companion agreed and suggested we meet at midday.

On my way home I wondered what I was getting into.

# BACK TO LLANDUDOCH

At midday on the next day I arrived at Llandudoch. It is a large village at the far north end of Pembrokeshire, very close to Cardigan. In fact for many years half the village was in the neighbouring county of Ceredigion. The name St Dogmaels is associated with the Welsh saint, Dogfael. Many stories and anecdotes are connected with this place. Here are two.

## THE WHITE LADY OF ST DOGMAEL'S

In the village church of St Dogmael's is a stone called the Sagranus Stone. Once it served as a footbridge across a stream in the village. The ghost of a lady in white was said to haunt the bridge.

## THE GOLDEN COFFIN

Once, long ago, an Irish Princess was buried in a golden coffin at St Dogmael's Abbey. It was said that anyone who ventured down the steps and into her tomb would be struck down dead.

I waited by the statue of the mermaid who saved the life of a local fisherman. It was from here that I clearly saw the 'bar', the barrier or spit of land at the mouth of the River Teifi which has caused much trouble for fishermen.

Somewhere in my rucksack was a copy of the poem by Alfred Lord Tennyson, which describes the 'bar'. I had remembered to put it there last night, but, oh dear why do I always cram so much stuff in? I had to tip it out on the ground, and then replace everything, before realising that I had put it in the pocket at the front. After all that, I hope the poem serves as an explanation of the 'bar'.

### Crossing the Bar

Sunset and evening star,
And one clear call for me!
And may there be no moaning of the bar,
When I put out to sea,

But such a tide as moving seems asleep,
Too full for sound and foam,
When that which drew from out the boundless deep
Turns again home.

Twilight and evening bell,
And after that the dark!
And may there be no sadness of farewell,
When I embark;

For though from out our bourne of Time and Place
The flood may bear me far,
I hope to see my Pilot face to face
When I have crost the bar.

When I looked up from the paper on which I had copied the poem I saw that the little man was there. He frowned at me: 'I hope I am not disturbing your paperwork?'

I apologised and asked if he would like to hear the story of Peregrine and the Mermaid. He sat down on the nearby seat and nodded. I sat next to him.

## PEREGRINE AND THE MERMAID

There was a fisherman named Peregrine who lived in a tiny terraced cottage at Cwmins, St Dogmaels. Like all fishermen of the day, he could forecast the weather quite accurately.

Once, he was fishing for herring near Pen Cemaes with his nets, even though his old *Mamgu* (Grandma) had warned him against fishing there. It was, she repeated many times, one of the only places in the whole world where the land of *Plant Rhys Dwfn* –the *Tylwyth Teg* – could be clearly seen. And it should be avoided. But Peregrine needed to bring back enough of a catch to feed his wife and himself, especially since his young wife was expecting their first child and needed good food. What's more, he needed extra fish to sell at the quayside and in the market.

He hauled in his nets and found he had more than just fish. He had caught a mermaid. Naturally she begged to be put back in the sea. The fisherman ignored her appeals, thinking that she could be useful to him. So he tied her up, and then headed back for St Dogmaels. But as he neared the 'bar', the great sand spit caused by the watery turmoil between sea and river at the estuary mouth, listening all the time to the crying and wailing of the mermaid, he finally took pity on her and released her into the sea.

She thanked him, and before swimming away, promised to inform Peregrine of any impending storms. He asked her how she would do that, but she told him to just wait and see.

When he arrived home, he showed his wife his catch of herring – some for supper, some to pickle, with money to be made in Cardigan from the sale of the rest of the catch. His wife was delighted.

Then he told her about the mermaid. She thought he was teasing her, but then she saw that he really was serious and rather worried too.

She was also worried. Her *Mamgu* had told her the stories about Pen Cemaes. If the *Tylwyth Teg* entered your home, they could, if they wished, cause all sorts of mischief, but worst of all it was said that they particularly like to get into a home with a small baby.

Then they would steal the baby and replace it with one of their own. The young wife was afraid for her unborn child and made her husband promise to cease fishing there.

On 30 September 1789, Peregrine was one of many fishermen in small boats setting out to make their living. When his boat reached the bar, the mermaid appeared alongside and warned him of the coming storm. Peregrine heeded the mermaid's warning and tried to persuade the other fishermen to return to St Dogmaels with him. They laughed and carried on out to sea. Peregrine and his boat and crew returned safely to St Dogmaels.

Later that day at the Tavern he was shocked to hear the news that:

A most melancholy catastrophe happened on Cardigan river between four and five o'clock this morning. The fishermen having taken up their nets with a great quantity of herrings, were lying under shelter between little quay (old lifeboat house) and Allt y Goed farm, waiting the turn of the tide to carry them in. The wind, being then south-west, blowing an easy gale. It suddenly changed to north-west and blew a sort of hurricane. A most tremendous storm ensued, the sea running mountains high and carrying everything before it and making the most terrific ravages. The fishing boats were dispersed and some thrown on the beach, some thrown on the rocks. Three more unfortunate than the rest overset and every man on board (except for four, who providentially saved themselves by swimming) were swallowed up by the savage elements to the number of 27. The same morning two boats with 15 men were lost at Newquay.

This was recorded on 1 October 1789 in St Dogmaels church records.

After this incident Peregrine always had an eye on the weather and the clouds. He rarely needed the warning of the mermaid.

☙ —❧

After the story, the little man nodded, pleased that some of the old stories survived.

We searched for the hairs of a mermaid that my companion required. It wasn't easy. He described the hair as very fine. We looked by the statue, under the seat on the green, and in amongst the flotsam and jetsam on the beach. I was unsure how we would find them and was reminded of something my mother once said about trying to find a needle in a haystack. I was about to suggest that maybe we should meet at one of the other places where mermaids had reportedly been seen, when I heard a shout of triumph. It came from the branches of a tree. He climbed down carrying a single, long, silvery hair which had a greenish hue. It was beautiful and even though there was just a single hair it seemed to reflect the colours of the sea. I took a tissue from my rucksack and we carefully wrapped the single hair to keep it safe. He put the small parcel inside his hat.

Then he told me another story from this place.

## KILLER TOADS OF CEMAES

In the late twelfth century there was a woodturner in Cemaes who made handles for tools. It was poorly paid work, but despite this he never seemed short of money. Some said he was a robber. He denied it, even to his wife, but never explained to her how he seemed to fare better than his neighbours. One night he was taken ill. He woke up in a sweat from a nightmare. But although he was awake, the nightmare didn't cease. His eyes stared and he screamed with pain and fear.

His wife treated him for a fever, but after several days the illness was no better. The wise woman was sent for. She came with herbs to treat his illness but he didn't get any better.

As well as a high fever, he kept complaining about huge toads nibbling away at his fingers, toes and nose. He would cry out in the middle of the night. His wife came to his bed, and sometimes when his cries were very loud, the neighbours came too. But no toads were seen. As he became weaker and weaker, all the cures that were brought for him were useless. He couldn't eat and found difficulty sleeping, and had a terror of being alone. So his wife, his brother and his cousin and several neighbours all took turns in sitting with him.

One night his brother was sitting beside his bed, keeping a lamp lit, when he heard a movement at the foot of the bed. He went to investigate and there was a toad, followed by another and yet another. After some time the floor was literally heaving with a mass of toads. They crawled over the sick man and nibbled his toes, his fingers and his nose and probably other parts of his body. The brother tried to beat them off. The wife came and tried to beat them off. The neighbours came to see what the fuss was about and saw the toads nibbling at the sick man, and him thrashing about in his sick bed trying to be rid of them. They all fought off the toads and became weary with the effort. Eventually a friend said that they needed to get him away from that place, to somewhere that the toads could not get him.

They stripped the bark and leaves from a tree to make it smooth and hard for toads to climb, then they hoisted him to the top of the tree in a large bag. At last he would be out of the way of the toads. But the toads did climb the tree, and ate the man. Nothing remained but a bag full of bones. Some shook their heads and said that this was his punishment for dishonesty, but who knows?

Before we said goodbye, I offered him a key which I had brought from the collection of old keys I had in the drawer of the kitchen table (Why do we keep old keys – because they might come in handy one day? They never do.) He looked at it, and then shook his head. It would not do. It was a particular key he wanted. I asked him to describe it – he couldn't. Then he spied my sketch book and pencils and he drew the key. Here is what he drew:

I was beginning to get concerned. The deadline for my book was looming. I should have been at home writing, not scouring the Pembrokeshire countryside for objects which were being demanded one at a time by a small man who didn't seem very grateful, and who behaved as if I was simply there to do his bidding.

But it was true that I had offered to help. It seemed churlish to withdraw the offer. Besides, the night before I had included the day's incidents in my writing and the words were flowing well. Almost like magic.

I sat down and thought very hard. I had seen a key similar to the one he drew. Then I remembered. I had often sat sketching near the Pentre Ifan Cromlech, an awe-inspiring place set in a beautiful landscape. Many artists have captured it over centuries. On one occasion I had been caught in the rain, packed my things quickly and dashed for shelter under a tree near a small house. I remembered that there was a potting shed in the garden of the house and I had noticed a key in the lock, very like the one he had drawn. I had been surprised at the time, because it was strangely large for a small shed.

I kept the information to myself and said I would meet the man by the ancient burial chamber the next day at the usual time. I decided to go on the mission for the key alone, as I was afraid that my companion would simply take the key without asking.

Before we parted I asked him something new. 'I would like to know your name. If I am to include these adventures in my book, I would like to refer to you by name.' I received a stubborn look in response. With his chin jutting out and a frown creasing his forehead he said nothing. I thought that perhaps he had not heard me, so I asked again, 'Please tell me your name.' Again the frown.

Finally he said, 'As a storyteller you should know that I can't tell you.' Then I watched him as he strode away.

# PENTRE IFAN

Pentre Ifan is a splendid burial chamber dating back to about 3,500 BC. It has a huge capstone of some 30 tons and is delicately poised on three uprights. There are other stones lying flat on the ground. They may once have stood upright. Today sheep graze nearby. In

spring they use these fallen stones for their favourite games of 'I'm the king of the castle', butting each other off and jumping into the air as if on springs. I believe it is called pronking or stotting.

Once, this cromlech was known as Arthur's Quoit; Pentre Ifan means Ivan's Village – a place of many names, whispered tales and restless winds. The high hillside on which it stands looks out to Newport Bay and the Irish Sea beyond. Perhaps on the clearest days you can see Ireland itself, another land of the people who built Pentre Ifan. Much closer is the distinctive profile of Carn Ingli, its slopes rising steadily to a sudden mountain-top cairn, fit for the angels for whom Carn Ingli is named. Sweeping down below Pentre Ifan, the dense oak woodlands of Cilrhydd shelter another world of grey-green lichens, mosses and violets, but up here on the restless hillside, it is the yellow flowers of gorse with their aroma of coconut that guard the rugged stones. Overhead, red kites swoop and tumble, reminding one who is really in charge around here.

It is said that those who had been interred under the great stone were closer to the Spirit World and also closer to the Sun, worshipped in many cultures as the giver of life, warmth and abundance.

The next day I knocked nervously at the door of the house close by the cromlech, where I had spied the key. The door was ajar and a voice within said: '*Dewch i mewn*' (please come in).

'Sorry,' I explained, stepping into the room. 'My Welsh is rather poor. I'm still learning and at my age it comes rather slowly.'

Despite the heat of the day, a log fire burned in the grate; the heat made me perspire and I felt my skin itch. Beside the fire sat an old woman, wrapped in a woollen shawl. Her hair was mostly silver but a few red hairs gave a glint echoed by the flames in the fire. Her eyes were green and surprisingly bright. She tutted crossly at me and pointed her bony finger at another chair on the other side of the fire and said, '*Eisteddwch i lawr*' (sit down).

She looked so cross at my lack of Welsh that I was almost afraid to ask about the key. But it was half-past eleven, and I had to meet the man at midday; I couldn't let him down. I decided to tell the woman the story of my companion, his troubles and the search for tokens or objects.

I was astonished at her lack of surprise. She looked at me with piercing eyes, then half-smiled and told me to help myself to the key. The lock was broken anyway and she said she would be pleased to help. I offered to pay for it and she started to look angry again. Then I offered to get a new lock fitted, but she said it wasn't necessary, anyone who wanted to steal the old bicycle and flower pots in the shed probably had more need of them than she did.

I thanked her in my halting Welsh, '*Diolch.*' She smiled. I went to the potting shed and took out the key. It was surprisingly rust free, despite its age and lack of use. I stood in her garden, in which grew many herbs and old-fashioned flowers. I drank in the sweet smell, reminded of what Waldo Williams, the Pembrokeshire poet, had said. Waldo was a Quaker and a poet in the Welsh tradition of the Cynghanedd.

Apparently, one day he had parked his old bike up against a butcher's shop in Haverfordwest. When he came out of the shop, the bike had been stolen. He had said that whoever took it probably had more need of it than he did, and continued his journey on foot.

When I finally left the old woman's house I had to run to the cromlech, as it was nearly midday and I didn't want to be late. I met my companion and triumphantly handed him the key. He was thrilled. He jumped up and down in delight. It was the very one! I told him about the kindness of the old woman. He said she was well known for her wisdom, and he told me a story about her.

## SIONED

Sioned (Janet) was a wise woman, who lived in her ancestral home within sight of the Pentre Ifan Cromlech. Many people came to her for a blessing on their union, their new baby or their relative's death. Some came for help or advice, as in earlier days many had come to her mother and grandmother in their own lifetimes.

Those seeking advice, wisdom or help were expected to bring a gift and then to sit and await wise counsel. Sometimes the waiting was so long that people slept in the *simne fawr* (inglenook) until Sioned was ready to speak. She would not be hurried. People knew that if she was put out of countenance she would shout and ask everyone to leave her home.

A young couple called Mair and Sam, already married four years, came to the home of Sioned to ask why there had been no child born to them. They brought a simple gift of a hand-carved wooden box, made by Sam, who was a craftsman. They knocked nervously at the door and waited. They saw that the door was ajar but they knew that it would be impolite to enter without being invited. They knew her reputation, so they waited in silence for what seemed like hours, but it was in fact only half an hour.

Whilst they waited, a neighbouring farmer drove his cows along the road outside, tipped his hat and gave what Mair thought was a knowing wink. She blushed to the roots of her dark curly hair. Sam smiled, thinking she looked especially pretty with this glow on her cheeks. Eventually they heard footsteps; the door creaked open further and there in the doorway stood the eldest woman that either of them had ever seen. They presented their gift and waited whilst she inspected it. They shuffled whilst they waited. The farmer walked back along the lane by the house, whistling, and gave them a 'knowing' look, which made Mair blush again.

Eventually the old woman opened the door wide and asked them in. They went into the high-ceilinged kitchen of the very old house which had been in Sioned's family for many centuries. The small windows let in very little light, making the room seem rather dark and dingy. There were spiders' webs hanging from the beams in this room, and Mair saw mouse droppings under the table. The old woman's cat eyed the young couple suspiciously as they removed piles of books and a basket containing a strange assortment of objects, to make room on two of the chairs. They sat down carefully, not wanting to appear so rude as to brush off the dust. They were, after all, wearing their Sunday best for this visit.

The old woman sat in her chair by the fire and looked at them with her piercing and surprisingly dark-green eyes. She pointed a long forefinger with its joints all swollen and a rather grubby nail, towards some cups on the dresser.

'The kettle has just boiled,' she said in a voice more youthful than they had expected.

Sam took three cups from hooks on the dresser. He picked up a clean cloth from a hook behind the door and rubbed the cups inside and out with it. Then he did the same with a jug taken from a hook on the same dresser. He took the jug to the churn just outside the door, ladled in some milk, and put the cups and milk on the table. The old woman looked at Mair and pointed at the teapot and the tea caddy. Mair put two caddy spoons of tea in the pot.

The old woman pointed again, saying, 'Three, put three.'

Mair counted three spoons of tea, while Sam took a knitted kettle holder from a hook above the fireplace. Mair placed the teapot on a trivet in the hearth, and Sam poured the boiling water on to the tea leaves. He saw a tea cosy hanging from the bressumer beam, which he placed on the teapot.

'Good,' said the old woman, 'needs to draw, get some sugar and a spoon.'

When the old woman was satisfied that the tea was ready, she indicated that they should pour. Sam poured three cups of tea and handed one to Sioned, and one to Mair. Sioned placed two spoonfuls of sugar from the sugar bowl into her cup and stirred for several minutes before staring long and hard at them both.

The young couple found the silence uncomfortable. It made the sound of the stirring seem very loud. Sam sipped his tea and watched the cat, which seemed to have been alerted by something under the old woman's chair. Mair sat on the edge of her chair looking pleadingly at Sam; she wanted to leave, but she had lost her nerve. She was uncomfortable about drinking the tea and concerned about the rather grubby, dusty house and the old woman who seemed to be able to stare right inside her.

She watched Sam as Sam watched the cat and the old woman watched them both. Finally the old woman noisily drank her cup of tea down to the last drop. She put her cup down on its saucer with a clatter, looked at Mair and Sam, then back at Mair, and then spoke.

Poor Mair nearly jumped out of her skin as the near-silence was broken. At the same time the cat leapt under the old woman's chair and came out with a mouse which she took outside through the door which had been left ajar, presumably for this very purpose.

'To have a child you must firstly love each other and I can see that you do. Next you must have wisdom beyond your years. I am happy that if you do not yet possess wisdom, you are both sensitive to what is needed and are able to learn quite quickly.'

Mair and Sam looked at each other, amazed at the perception of the old woman. They had not explained or even been asked about their needs, or about why they had come. They had both anticipated a lengthy interview, but hardly any words had been exchanged.

Mair then understood that the whole business of making tea had been Sioned's way of observing how they were together, how they responded to unspoken requests, the sensitivity with which they adapted to each other's needs. She smiled; Sam still seemed puzzled, but she could explain later.

The old woman gave a nod and a smile, and continued: 'I cannot directly help you, but the *Rhys Plant* (little people) may. If you make a suitable gift, and I can see Sam that you are quite a craftsman, make something of suitable size, wait until the moon is full, go together and place it on the south side of the cromlech. Wait there until you hear the owl or fox. Then go home and carry on with your usual lives. I can't make any promises but it is worth a try.'

'Is that it?' Sam tried to keep the scorn from his voice. 'No secret potion or ritual, just a gift and wait for the fairies?'

'I can see you are sceptical, perhaps you should listen more to your mother and grandmother: they know – and she knows.' The old woman nodded at Mair.

Mair blushed again. 'Sam and his friends do not believe in the old ways. They think that fairies and spirits are an invention of parents and grandparents, designed to keep children in order.'

Sioned shook her head. 'Spirits and fairies exist all round us, invisible. Fairies have no solid bodily substance. Their forms are of matter like ghostly bodies, and they cannot be caught. In the twilight they are often seen, and on moonlight nights in summer. Only certain people can see fairies, and such people hold communication with them and have dealings with them, but it is difficult to get them to talk about fairies.

'My mother used to tell about seeing the "fair-folk" dancing in the fields near Cardigan; and other people have seen them round the cromlech up there on the hill [the Pentre Ifan Cromlech]. They appeared as little children in clothes like soldiers' clothes, and with red caps, according to some accounts. You, Sam, who scorn the old ways, do as I say and just wait and see.'

That was it. Sioned settled back in her chair. After a few minutes she started to snore. Mair and Sam got up quietly and washed and put away the crocks. Then they stealthily let themselves out, leaving the door ajar, just as they had found it.

As they walked home they discussed what had been said. Although Sam was sceptical he was impressed that the old woman knew why they'd come without asking. He decided that he would make

a wooden box and go with Mair, when the moon was full, to the cromlech and take the gift.

Three months after the gift was made Sam could tell by the light in Mair's eyes that she had good news. They took the gift of a cake, baked by Mair, to the old woman. Some months later a boy was born to them. He was small, but her mother said that was on account of being early. Mair and Sam were so grateful to Sioned and to the little people that every year on the little boy's birthday they made two small gifts. One for the old woman, and one which was left on the south side of the cromlech.

The two of us – my strange companion and I – were sitting facing the cromlech where Sam had left his gifts. I read to my companion from the notes of W.Y. Evans Wentz, an Edwardian collector of Celtic beliefs:

> The region, the little valley on whose side stands the Pentre Ifan Cromlech, the finest in Britain, is believed to have been a favourite place with the ancient Druids. And in the oak groves (Ty Canol Wood) that still exist there, tradition says there was once a flourishing school for neophytes, and that the Cromlech instead of being a place for internments or sacrifices was in those days completely enclosed, forming, like other Cromlechs, a darkened chamber in which novices, when initiated were placed for a certain number of days. The interior (of Pentre Ifan) being called the womb or court of Ceridwen.

He nodded his head slowly and thoughtfully, looked at me as if making a decision. Then he shook his head, as if I was not ready to hear what he had to say. He asked me, 'Have you guessed?' I shook my head, and he looked disappointed. But he shrugged his shoulders, and told me another story about this place.

# SUDDEN RICHES

Two hundred or more years ago there was a landowner called Evans who lived in a large and beautifully appointed house, surrounded by woodland and with lovely gardens. Mrs Evans strove to ensure that the house was kept in splendid order, directing the servants in their activities and ensuring that the curtains, cushions and hangings were cleaned each spring and replaced when they became unfashionable. Her wardrobe too reflected her status as a wealthy landowner's wife, with many dresses of silk, satin, lawn and velvet, decorated with lace, beads and jewels.

Evans was pleased that his wife enhanced his status; she looked quite the lady of the manor. Their house was fit for a lord, and they entertained in grand style. He was, however, concerned that his income was insufficient to keep up appearances. Some of the tradespeople and other creditors had to wait overly long for payment of their bills.

He tried on many occasions to get his wife to cut down on their expenses, but she said it was impossible, she didn't know how. She also went into a dreadful sulk at these times, storming out of the room, slamming the door and refusing to speak for days on end. He also noticed that his meals (and only his) became very frugal after asking his wife to economise. A plate hardly able to sustain a child, let alone a grown man, was placed in the library so that he could eat alone, whilst the rest of the family enjoyed much better fare in the dining room.

He tried to get his wife to reduce the purchase of furnishings and gowns. After these sessions his wife put out the most ragged clothes she could find for him and the children and she went to visit her mother, until he pleaded with her to come home.

He soon learnt that his home life was happier, his wife was more loving, his food more delicious and the children happier when he let her have free rein with household purchases. Thereafter he tried to cut corners with the work on the land, paying less for labour, buying poor quality seed and animal fodder. The result was that his best workers went to work for a neighbouring landowner, his crops failed, and his animals were prey to disease and neither bred nor worked well.

But the creditors still needed paying, and he became frantic. One evening he shut himself in the study with a bottle of brandy and drank rather too much of it. Afterwards he let himself out of the house and went for a walk to clear his head and to think things through.

His walk took him along the lane into the woodland. He walked the well-trodden track, listening to the noises of the night: owls, foxes, badgers and all manner of rustling and pattering of feet. Under a bright moon, he continued his walk until he came to the ancient cromlech of Pentre Ifan.

As he approached he heard voices, and so moved slowly and quietly. He crouched down behind a gorse bush and watched. There, bathed in moonlight were small people, some smaller than his youngest child, who had only just learned how to walk; little people apparently wearing soldiers' clothes, with red caps. He watched them dancing in the moonlight, played by fairy fiddlers and pipers. He was transfixed.

When the dancing stopped the small people sat at tables to eat and drink and sing. As he watched, someone shook him by the elbow. He was terrified – everyone knew that if the small people caught you looking at their festivities it could mean certain death. The hairs on the back of his neck prickled. He slowly turned his head to see an old man dressed in old-fashioned clothes, with skin that looked translucent, without life.

The old man spoke. 'Come back to this place tomorrow and dig a hole in the place where they have danced. Take home what you find, and keep it in a safe and secret place. Your luck will change and your only payment will be to make an offering of something from the land at this place once a year.' He then disappeared into thin air.

Evans crept away from there. He worried when a dry twig snapped that the small people would discover him. But they were laughing and singing so much at their feast table that they didn't hear him.

He slept so well that night, relieved that he had not been discovered by the little folk, pleased at the information given to him by the strange old man. Perhaps his worries and troubles would cease.

The next day he rose very early, worried that someone else would get there first. He took a shovel and a sack, telling his manservant that he was going to test the soil at the edge of the wood. He walked swiftly to the spot by the Pentre Ifan Cromlech, where the small people had danced the night before. There were tiny footprints there. If he hadn't observed the festivities the night before, he might have thought that the ground had been trampled by badgers.

He dug in the middle of the disturbed ground. It was surprisingly loose and easy to dig. After several spadefuls of earth had been removed, he found a box. He drew it out of the ground. It was heavy and clearly contained something. He couldn't open it because the clasp and hinges were rusty. He put the box in the sack he had brought for the purpose, and walked home.

In his study he took the sack and its contents and put it on a ledge inside the chimney, left the room, locking the door behind him, and made his way to the stables. There were tools and a forge there for small repairs. He selected an oil can and made his way back along the corridor. The head groom gave him a quizzical look. Usually the master would do anything to avoid getting his hands dirty.

At his desk, Evans spread out an oil cloth, then bathed the clasp and hinges of the box in oil, wrapped it in the sack and put it back into its hiding place, to await the freeing of the metal parts. Then he could, hopefully, open the box and discover its secrets.

The next day a letter arrived from a lawyer. Evans took his time in opening it, thinking that one of his creditors had become tired of waiting for his money. Finally he summoned up sufficient courage to break the seal and open the letter.

Lo and behold it was a lawyer informing him that a distant relative, with no wife, children or close family had died leaving him his entire estate: a considerable amount of money and property in the next county.

That season his cows gave unusually good and plentiful milk, and the hens laid really well with no moulting, each giving an egg a day without ceasing. The pigs grew so fat that there was more than enough pork for the family meals and some to hang in the chimney to smoke for ham. Their litters of piglets all survived well enough to fatten for the next season, with plenty to sell at market. The sheep all had healthy lambs – many with twins; and the fleeces were of such high quality that the weavers and spinners almost fought over the right to buy them.

The orchard grew apples and plums sufficient for puddings, plentiful jam and enough to ferment for cider and wine. Other crops were abundant. All the bills were paid, and there were no creditors haranguing him for payment of their bill. He started to have money in the bank; even his wife found it difficult to spend it all. He increased the wages of his workers, while others started to come back to work for him, and always there was a queue of people seeking work at his gate. He couldn't believe his luck. Then he remembered the box and his night by the cromlech. He still hadn't discovered the contents!

That evening he, his wife and children and some friends had a jolly evening with good food and plenty to drink and music and dancing. After supper he excused himself, saying that he had a pressing matter to deal with. He made his way to the study, took the box from the ledge inside the chimney, put it on the oil cloth on his desk and attempted to open it. The oil had done its work, the clasp and hinges were free and he was able to open the box.

The contents were wrapped in hessian, inside which was a layer of velvet. He unwrapped the velvet to reveal a gold figurine, very old, some sort of idol, but nothing recognisable. He cleaned the figurine, then wrapped it carefully again and replaced it in the box, which he put back on the ledge in the chimney.

This figurine was lucky. Since he found it, his luck had changed, just as the mysterious figure that night had predicted. He was going to keep it safe and keep the luck.

That winter the servants were surprised that he forbade a fire in his study. In the spring he had the blacksmith come and install a heavy safe in the wall of the study. In the safe he placed the box containing the figurine, and some of the money earned from the land. No one commented on the installation of the safe; after all the family was becoming very wealthy. Sometimes his wife was puzzled that he carried the key to the safe everywhere he went and only took off the chain holding the key from around his neck last thing at night, when he put it under his pillow.

Every year he placed something at Pentre Ifan where he had seen the dance and found the figurine. One year it was a basket woven from the willow trees, another year it was a corn dolly, then a pot made from clay dug from the land and fired in the kitchen fireplace. He used his ingenuity to create something new each year.

In the process of making these offerings he discovered new talents, which gave him a sense of satisfaction. Sometimes he employed craftsmen and women. Sometimes the children helped to create tokens. The important thing was that everything had to be made from something that came from their own land. Only his eldest daughter was given the secret. She knew the eventual destination for their efforts. She only knew because one night she was curious and followed him, but that's another story.

When Evans died, he left a rich estate to his family: £50,000 was a lot of money in those days. His daughter, who was now the keeper of the safe key, continued to leave the gifts once a year.

Who knows if the practice continued? Who knows if the family still exists, let alone still shares the good luck given to Evans on that night centuries ago.

What I can tell you is that last time I visited the cromlech at Pentre Ifan, there was a posy of flowers left on the grass in front of the ancient monument.

On my way home I thought about yet another anecdote from this special place and one that is close to my heart since it concerns one of the many sacred wells of Wales.

## SACRED WELL

Once, not so long ago, a writer, who was gathering material for a book on the sacred wells of Wales, was visiting Pentre Ifan, having heard that one of Pembrokeshire's wells was close to the ancient monument. He searched in the usual places, at the corners of fields and settlements, and by hedge-banks, but failed to find the place. As evening approached and the light failed he decided to return to the inn at Nevern. He would have a meal and an early night, then try again in the morning. After a hearty steak and ale pie, followed by steamed pudding with treacle, he sat by the crackling log fire with a pint of beer, warming it in his hands. At the other side of the fireplace in a rocking chair sat an old man who greeted him: '*Noswaith dda, sut 'da chi?*'

'Sorry, I am from Cardiff, I don't speak Welsh,' said our writer.

The old man repeated his greeting in English: 'Good evening, how are you?'

'Well, thank you, but tired.' He then explained about the well and his search. The old man explained that there was no such place. The writer was astounded. He had studied source material which definitely described the well in this place.

Then the old man asked the writer if, at twilight, he had seen any 'old people' up there. Thinking that the man was teasing him and playing along with him, the writer bought him a pint, drew his chair a little closer and said: 'No, but I did see the Good People (faeries)'. The old man relented, laughed and arranged to take the writer to the well on the very next morning.

After breakfast the writer met the old man who took him up the lane to the missing well, which was easy to find, just under a hedge-bank, close to the cromlech.

The writer asked the old man why he had teased him the evening before. He explained that like his father and grandfather, he was the guardian of the well. He was afraid that the writer was an inspector from the water company, checking licences for drawing domestic water from natural springs. He realised that a water inspector would probably not believe in faeries.

The following poem by Waldo Williams is in celebration of Pentre Ifan:

### Cofio

Un funud fach cyn elo'r haul o'r wybren,
Un funud fwyn cyn delo'r hwyr i'w hynt,
I gofio am y pethau anghofiedig
Ar goll yn awr yn llwch yr amser gynt.

Fel ewyn ton a dyr ar draethell unig,
Fel cân y gwynt lle nid oes glust a glyw,
Mi wn eu bod yn galw'n ofer arnom –
Hen bethau anghofiedig dynol ryw.

Camp a chelfyddyd y cenhedloedd cynnar,
Aneddau bychain a neuaddau mawr,
Y chwedlau cain a chwalwyd ers canrifoedd
Y duwiau na ŵyr neb amdanynt 'nawr.

A geiriau bach hen ieithoedd diflanedig,
Hoyw yng ngenau dynion oeddynt hwy,
A thlws i'r clust ym mharabl plant bychain,
Ond tafod neb ni eilw arnynt mwy.

O, genedlaethau dirifedi daear,
A'u breuddwyd dwyfol a'u dwyfoldeb brau,
A erys ond tawelwch i'r calonnau
Fu gynt yn llawenychu a thristáu?

Mynych ym mrig yr hwyr, a mi yn unig,
Daw hiraeth am eich 'nabod chwi bob un;
A oes a'ch deil o hyd mewn Côf a Chalon,
Hen bethau anghofiedig teulu dyn?

This translation is by Tony Conran:

### Remembering

Before the sun has left the sky, one minute,
One dear minute, before the journeying night,
To call to mind the things that are forgotten
Now in the dust of ages lost from sight.

Like foam of a wave on a lonely seacoast breaking,
Like the wind's song where there's no ear to mind,
I know they're calling, calling to us vainly –
Old unremembered things of humankind.

Exploit and skill of early generations,
From tiny cottages or mighty hall,
Fine tales that centuries ago were scattered,
The gods that nobody knows now at all.

Little words of old, fugitive languages
That were sprightly on the lips of men
And pretty to the ear in the prattle of children –
But no one's tongue will call on them again.

Oh, generations on the earth unnumbered,
Their divine dreams, fragile divinity –
Is only silence left to the heart's affections
That once rejoiced and grieved as much as we?

Often when I'm alone and it's near nightfall,
I yearn to acknowledge you and know each one.
Is there no way fond memory can keep you,
Forgotten ancient things of the family of man?

We arranged to meet in Moylgrove the next day, on the bridge over the river, Nant Ceibwr. The next thing on my companion's list was a box. 'You are not to bother about that. I know where to get the very one. It is not far from there.' I didn't dare ask.

He also asked me to bring a basket so that he could carry the growing number of objects we had collected. I asked if it had to be a particular basket. He looked scornfully at me and said, 'of course not'. Then he looked at me again and said: 'Well have you guessed?' I looked quizzically at him. He shook his head and walked away.

As I made my way home the penny finally dropped; the reason why he couldn't tell me his name, the reason why I, as a storyteller should know: just as in the tale of Rumpelstiltskin, it was for me to guess. That was why he kept asking.

Oh dear, I should have known! So I spent some time that evening, thinking of names that would be relevant. I thought about the way he looked, what he wore, I thought about the things we had collected so far. I couldn't find a clue.

# TREWYDDEL, MOYLGROVE

I continued my thoughts the next day as I waited, sitting on the bridge by the river. I was envious of the well-kept gardens of the house next to the bridge. Colourful flower borders, magnificent trees and shrubs, and a small summer house. My own garden was suffering from neglect. The sound of water rushing by underneath put me in something of a reverie. I closed my eyes to think more clearly about the conundrum of my companion's name. The next thing I knew was an impatient tapping on my shoulder. 'No time for sleeping,' said the man. He told me about this village.

No one is quite sure how the village got its name. Elderly residents say that the church was once called the Church of Matilda's Grove. The Welsh for Matilda is Mallt, which is associated with a number of rather eerie legends.

## MALLT OF THE MIST

If you are walking home from the pub on a foggy night, be warned: if you see Mallt, also known as *Y Mwnci Mallt*, or Mallt of the Mist at the end of the lane to Penrallt Ceibwr washing her hands in a woodland stream, then, it is said, you will die.

Mallt of the Mist is a fleet-footed hunter, usually seen with two black hounds beside her on a leash, and behind her a creature, half hound, half wolf. She is often to be found in the court of the *Brenin Llwyd* or Grey King, in his court of the mist.

Sometimes she is accompanied by another Matilda, *Mallt y Nos* or Matilda of the Night, a hag who uses an evil force to drive the dogs onwards. They ride on coal-black horses, with fiery eyes that turn white with heat, like furnaces. Their hunting crops are of red-hot iron, while the bridles and reins are made of steel.

It is said that many years ago a man – let us call him Bryn – happened upon these two evil women and their hounds. He followed them and was never seen again. The wise women in Moylgrove warn that if any person joins the procession of hags and dogs, blood falls in showers like rain, human bodies are torn to pieces and death soon follows the victims of the nocturnal expedition.

A favourite meeting place was the crossroads, sometimes around graves, when the spirits of the dead visited their last resting place. Another was the grove, where grew the mandrake – a plant of powerful magic. When the feet of the hounds touched the mandrake plant it screamed out loud. The hounds left their uncanny traces in the shape of human bones amidst torn-up turf and lumps of earth, which, when trodden upon, emitted a flame, with a strong smell of sulphur.

Sometimes the hags and dogs were known to pursue people who would then be doomed to die within twelve months. At such times they went quietly, stealthily, without so much as a faint cry to announce their approach. They were seen but not heard as they pursued their victim from room to room in ancient mansion or humble cottage. The spirits of those pursued were seen running out into the night, followed by the hideous hounds.

My companion told me about another Matilda of the night.

## Mallt y Nos

There was once a beautiful woman who married and moved to this part of Wales from Gloucestershire to join her husband in his home.

She was passionate about riding with hounds. Her new husband thought she spent too much time in the saddle, and not enough looking after his needs. He made her promise to give up hunting. She was so in love that she was prepared to give up her passion for hunting in favour of her passion for him. For more than two years she honoured that promise, and perhaps all would have been well if he had not had to go away for a considerable time.

During his absence his wife could not resist the temptation of the chase. She had her favourite horse saddled and rode away to a meet. She met up with friends and asked them to keep her secret. She followed the hounds for a whole day having some exciting sport. On her way home in the twilight her horse threw her. When her husband returned he found his wife nursing a broken leg. He guessed the reason and was furious and upset that she had broken her promise.

He sought the advice of a local *dyn hysbys*, a seer well-informed in matters that are dark to others. This man recited incantations which threw the wife into the courtyard where she was seized by a whirlwind, carried away and was doomed to ride on the storm for all eternity. Her soul was to join *Arawn* and his *Cŵn Annwn* (hounds of the underworld) and the fiery steeds. She is fated ti hunt until the end of time. Her cries are sad and pitiful as she runs low beside the spirit hounds or takes an aerial flight with the *Cŵn Wybyr* (hounds of the sky). She is sometimes seen astride a fiery steed riding through lonely villages in winter.

I then told a story of more recent times.

### The Tithe War

There was once a woman called Pegi Lewis. She was attracted to a handsome young boy called Morgan, who worked for her father Dafydd Lewis y Crudd on their farm in Moylgrove.

She would often time her walks across the farmyard to coincide with Morgan's return from the fields. She took time and trouble over her appearance, often getting into trouble with her mother. When Morgan came into the kitchen for meals she made sure that he got the tastiest morsels and that he understood that she had cooked them. He found her company pleasant, and was thrilled at the attention. He brought her small gifts, and read her poetry. Eventually the young couple fell in love and married.

Some months later a letter came. Morgan's father, a widower, with no other children, had become too ill to manage the family farm. So, the newlyweds left Moylgrove for Whitland to manage Morgan's family farm and to look after his elderly father. The journey there was long and hard.

Having set up home in her husband's place, Pegi didn't have many opportunities to return home. She missed her family and her old home. She missed the sea. But she was happy with Morgan and his father wasn't too difficult.

After several happy but hard-working months Pegi gave birth to a lovely baby boy. They named him Harri. The only sadness was that her mother could not make the long journey to Whitland to greet her new grandson.

Some months after the birth of Harri, Pegi made her first journey home to Moylgrove. The reason for her return was a funeral, following the death of her mother. Despite the sad occasion, everyone in the village was pleased to see her and to meet the new member of the family. After the funeral she went back to Whitland and her husband, who had really missed both his wife and his son.

Months went by and she gave birth to a daughter; they called her Mary. With the work on the family farm in Whitland and two children to look after, Pegi could only rely on the post to keep in touch with her father. She didn't see him decline in health.

Her father found it difficult to manage, but he didn't want to bother Pegi. First he sold the pig to a neighbour to buy some feed for the cows. After a few months he sold the other farm animals to pay his taxes, keeping only one cow. Then the fields were sold one by one. All that remained was the farmhouse, a small strip of land around it and the cow.

A neighbour saw the decline of the man and the farm and got in touch with Pegi. She came as quickly as she could and was shocked to see the state of her father's health and the decimation of the farm.

She cleaned up as best she could and tried to manage the pile of bills and letters that had been gathering dust on the dresser. It was terrible. Lots of money was due and there was almost nothing left: no money and no land. The only animal left was the cow.

Then, to crown it all, a bailiff came for tithes. Farmers were expected to pay a proportion of their harvest and yield in taxes to the church. All the farmers in the county were struggling to pay these tithes; it was an unfair tax, paid to a church they didn't attend. Many refused – there was anger and many arrests.

Farmers who refused to pay their tithes were subject to enforced sales of their stock to pay their debts. These sales were obstructed in many ways by those who opposed payment. Gates to farms would be locked, or large boulders or hawthorn bushes would block the way to the sale. The 'Tithe Horn' would be sounded by the farmer to summon help from his neighbours to deter the officials from carrying out their duty.

Pegi looked around the farm that her father and mother had worked so hard for all their lives. The only thing left to show for their hard labours was a cow. This was Pegi's inheritance. She was angry.

Her father wasn't the only one to be financially crippled by this unfair tax. She determined to fox the bailiffs. She stood her ground. When the neighbours told her that the bailiffs were on their way, she opened the field gate, allowing her beast to go free. Needless to say the official from the court was unable to catch this cow and went away empty-handed.

The man nodded his head in approval. Like me, he enjoyed mischief, especially when it played tricks on pompous people or officials. I asked him what to bring on the following day. My companion said: 'tomorrow we meet at the churchyard in Nevern. Bring milk.'

# NANHYFER, NEVERN

We met as arranged. I had been in this remarkable churchyard before, and looked up at the tall carved Celtic cross. I had not remembered just how tall it is, but, this time, seeing my friend of small stature beside it was startling.

I brought a flask of fresh organic milk which I was given at Penrhiw, the organic dairy farm on Pencaer. He took it and drank the lot. I started to protest but he gave me a withering look, and then settled down to tell me about this place.

# THE BLEEDING YEW

In Nevern Churchyard there is an ancient yew tree which 'bleeds' an unidentifiable red liquid that has baffled scientists and arborists for years. The legend states that a man was hanged from this tree and it has been bleeding ever since. It also states that the tree will continue to bleed until a Welshman sits on the throne in Nevern Castle.

# THE CUCKOO

Brynach's feast day was April 7th. On this day, the cuckoo would fly back and perch on the great Celtic cross, which was the signal that spring had arrived. One year the cuckoo was late. When it eventually appeared the poor bird was so exhausted after its long flight that it dropped down dead. According to the legend it had battled its way through storms to reach the church because it knew it could not fail its ancestors who had the honour of sounding spring's arrival on St Brynach's day.

# GLIMPSES

Sightings of small people, a phantom horseman and a *Ladi Wen* or 'White Lady' have all been reported from Pentre Ifan and the surrounding area. Some talk of mysterious 'black dogs', large 'black cats' and even a lion being spotted. 'Earthlights' have been reported from the village of Nevern. Older people in the village said they knew about them as children. They called them 'corpse candles' and they were an omen of death.

Nevern and the Gwaun valley are famous for their wise men and women called 'the knowing ones'. Their extensive herbal knowledge gave them healing powers, and a particular way with animals. Reportedly they could also summon spirits and put a hex on those who troubled them.

Mrs Betty Davies, a widow, lived in the early twentieth century, in a cottage by the bridge in Nevern; she was known as *Beti Pont Newydd*. Her three sons were at sea, and she missed them. One night she heard a knock at the door, and heard the voice of her eldest son calling 'Mother'. She went to the door and opened it wide, expecting to welcome her son whom she hadn't seen for many years. But she saw no one there. She went outside to make sure, and then sadly closed the door.

The next day she received the news that her eldest son, the one whose voice was heard, had been drowned at sea during the night.

No sooner had she recovered from the shock of the death of the first son than the same thing happened. This time she heard the voice of her second son. There was no one there when she opened the door. That very day she learned that her second son had also perished at sea.

Several years later she was found on the doorstep of a neighbour's house, crying. When they brought her inside and sat her down with a cup of tea she told them that: 'George is gone now too. He called me last night.' That very day the report of her third son being lost at sea was brought to her.

My friend told me that he had heard about another 'fore hearing'. Old Mrs Williams lived in the village, and had a younger sister whose baby was very sick. She was in a critical state and required much nursing. The whole household was tired and upset. Mrs Williams stayed with her sister to help out.

One afternoon, after a very disturbed night, Mrs Williams was trying to catch up on some lost sleep, when she heard the sound of creaking shoes passing hurriedly up and down the stairs. She got up, found her sister and asked if the baby was worse since she had heard lots of rushing up and down the stairs.

'What? No one has been here, no one has moved up or down the stairs, you must have been dreaming.' The mother's eyes were wide with fear.

'I was not dreaming,' said Mrs Williams, a bit put out. 'I was not even asleep. In fact I am so tired that I am returning home to catch up on my sleep.'

She returned to her own home. But a few days later, a messenger called for her, saying that the child was worse, and her help was needed. She hastily put on her Sunday best boots, which were hard and creaking.

When she reached her sister's she was asked to go for the doctor at once. She ran down the road, brought him to the house, and accompanied him upstairs. Then she went down again to fetch a bowl, then upstairs again, then down, then up again. On her last upstairs climb she found the baby dead.

Messengers were sent to tell the news to friends and family. Then she sank down into a chair to recover. Recalling the creaking boots and the sound of hurrying, troubled footsteps a few days beforehand, she realised that she had 'fore heard' the child's death.

It made my flesh creep to think that many strange sounds heard in the night could be a portent of danger or an ill omen. I hoped that my frequent bouts of insomnia wouldn't increase after hearing about 'fore telling'. Thinking of sleep – or lack of it – put me in mind of Carn Ingli, high above Nevern, the mountain where (if you are brave enough to spend the night) your dreams will be strange and wonderful. So I told my companion the tale of a man who spent not one night on Carn Ingli but forty years.

## Brynach

Once there was a man called *Brynach Wyddel* (Brynach the Irishman). He had travelled to Wales from Ireland, after being cast aside by the woman he loved. Reaching the Pembrokeshire coast, he made his way to Carn Ingli (Mount of Angels), to ask the spirits for their wisdom and guidance.

He lived alone for forty years on the magic mountain, surviving only on water from the sacred spring. It is said that in this time he journeyed to the underworld in Ceridwen's cauldron of inspiration and transformation.

After forty years, Brynach was told by the spirits to leave the mountain. He walked until he came to a beautiful river valley. Here in a still place, surrounded by ancient yews, Brynach came upon

Ceridwen, in the form of a Great White Sow. She gave him the gift of a wolf and also the ability to tame beasts. He was now master of a tame wolf, two magical stags, and a cow which produced a limitless supply of milk.

I stirred on the hard stone seat, having been sitting for just a bit too long. The avenue of yews in the churchyard at Nevern makes it dark even on a bright day. By now the sun was behind Carn Ingli, and the shadows in the churchyard were gloomier. But instead of ending our storytelling for the day, my friend now launched into one of the greatest tales from ancient Wales.

He started: 'If you should happen to visit Nevern on a feast day, you may just catch a glimpse of Ceridwen, the Goddess of the people of Wales, the guardian of the underworld and keeper of souls. She stirs her cauldron still, guarding her secret magical elixir in this sacred place, against those who would seek to win her secrets without love for her in their hearts. She is sometimes depicted as a Great White Sow. Many stories were told of the battles to catch, tame and defeat this creature and to steal her gifts. The greatest is from the Mabinogion.'

## CULHWCH AND OLWEN

Once upon a time there was a young prince called Culhwch. It had been predicted that he would never marry until he could win the hand of Olwen of the white footprints, daughter of Ysbaddaden Pencawr (called Thornogre in many versions of the story). He was the cheif of the giants. Culhwch's heart was captured by her very name, and he was determined to seek her out.

By now it was completely dark. An owl hooted above us and a blackbird sang his goodnight song. My friend stopped and said it was too late to tell the story now, but he would make sure that I heard it another time.

We sat for a while, listening to the sounds of the night. The peace was suddenly broken when my companion demanded, 'Have you guessed?'

When I looked blankly at him, he shook his head again sadly. It was a bit like the end of term interview with the headteacher; the one with the words, 'could do better'. Then my companion informed me that the next object on his list was a ring. The place where it must be handed over was Mynydd Preseli, the Preseli Hills. As he drew what he wanted, I thought about the many stories which contained rings. One of my favourites is the ring that Aladdin's uncle gave him, and which rendered him invisible when he wore it.

He passed his drawing over to me. 'I can't see a thing, it's too dark!' My friend stood up, walked to a far corner of the churchyard, and crouched down again. I followed him over, and saw that his face was glowing with a faint yellowish light from the ground. Glow worms! I took the drawing and held it close to the light. I could just make out the picture, and I was astonished. 'I have one just like this at home! It was my mother's.' I had a sentimental attachment to it, and was not keen to give it up. How was I going to deal with this?

My friend was clearly not bothered by my concerns. 'We will meet at Bwlch Gwynt – just by the plaque.'

I looked the ring out when I got home and had to think very hard about it. I recalled another ring – my mother's engagement ring – which had come to me after she died. It was subsequently stolen, and my brother and sister were angry that I hadn't taken better care of it.

Now I was contemplating giving away another of her rings. If I told my family, they would probably think that I was losing my senses. Little men and standing stones, and magic and fairies. I decided to keep quiet about it. I never wore the ring and I felt sure that my mother would have approved of it being used to help someone. I wrapped it in a fine cotton handkercheif, one of several kept in a box which had belonged to her.

# MYNYDD PRESELI

Bwlch Gwynt is one of the highest mountain passes in Wales, and from the top it seems you can view the whole of Pembrokeshire, as well as Snowdonia in the far north and Ireland in the west. Not a good place on a windy day. But this day was misty and calm. The only sounds were of lambs calling for their mothers as they grazed the mountain side. Many years ago these peaceful hills were the scene of a fierce local campaign to prevent the land being taken for military use. Today Preseli still belongs only to sheep, buzzards and the community of shepherds.

As I stood reading the plaque at Bwlch Gwynt commemorating this story, my companion, as ever, suddenly appeared from nowhere. Strange up here, where there was no cover, nowhere to hide, just the open rolling hills.

I handed over the ring wrapped in the handkerchief. He kept them both, and as payment he told me the story of Einion.

## MAMGU

Once, a poor shepherd boy called Einion tended sheep on the Preseli Hills.

One morning he was on his way to tend his flock when the cloud, mist and fog became so bad that he lost his way, even though he knew these mountains like the back of his hand. He wandered around for many hours, until eventually he came upon a hollow. He decided to sit, eat the food that he had brought with him, and wait until the mist cleared.

After he had eaten, he saw that the ground, where he had been sitting, had many grassy rings and he became afraid. His mamgu (grandma) had told him of the danger of fairy rings and of shepherds who had wandered into them and never been seen again. He tried to run away but the fog was so dense that he kept stumbling and couldn't find his way out of that place. He sat on a large stone panting with fear. Suddenly an old man appeared from out of the fog. The shepherd boy was more relieved than fearful, although the old man said nothing and simply walked past.

The boy decided that he would follow, because the old man looked as if he knew where he was going. They walked in silence for several miles. Suddenly the old man turned round and told Einion not to speak until he was given permission. Einion nodded his agreement, but became quite frightened. Nevertheless he followed the old man along the mountain path.

Eventually they came to a standing stone. Einion's eyes were wide with wonder and fear as he watched the old man walk up to the stone and tap it three times. Then, despite its weight and size, he lifted the stone effortlessly to reveal a pathway with stone steps winding down into the earth. The old man signalled to Einion to follow. He wanted to run away, but he was lost. Perhaps the old man was leading him home?

He followed the old man down the steps and along a dark tunnel. At the end of the tunnel they came out into beautiful woodland with many trees, birds and rivers. They continued walking until they came to a fine palace. The old man led him inside. It was richly decorated with much gold and silver. The floors were white marble. There was music coming from every room although no musicians were evident. In fact Einion saw no one else as he walked along the corridors.

They came to a banqueting hall where the table was laden with delicious food. Einion waited; his grandma had always told him to wait to be invited to eat at anyone's table. But where were the people? Even the old man had disappeared. He waited. He was hungry, the food smelled delicious, and he decided that it would be bad manners to let it go cold. He approached the table. One place had been set.

He sat down and ate a wonderful meal and polished it off with two glasses of wine. Afterwards he sat back, full of good food and warm from the wine and was astonished to see the food and the dishes and bottles vanish. As he sat, he heard voices and went to explore. He saw no one, but found a room where the door was open, a bed made with the cover turned down invitingly and a candle lit. He undressed and got into the bed; he found it very comfortable. The candle extinguished itself and he fell asleep.

The next day more food appeared; so he ate and drank a good breakfast, lunch and evening meal. His bed was made ready with the candle lit on the table beside the bed, but he didn't see another soul. Three days went by like this.

The old man reappeared. He told Einion that he could now speak. He tried to ask the old man many questions about where he was; where were the other people; where did the voices and the music come from; who prepared his food and his bed. But when he opened his mouth he found that he was unable to speak. His tongue became stuck fast to the roof of his mouth and would not move.

He was even more afraid for his safety than he had been at any other time of this adventure. Suddenly the door opened and an old woman entered the room, followed by three beautiful young women. They all started to ask Einion questions, but he was unable to answer. They saw that he was unable to reply and one of the young women kissed him gently on the lips, which loosened his tongue. He talked of his adventures, and the young women told of their lives. There was food, music, dancing and singing, and the feast went on into the night. The next day they took him through the many rooms of the palace and showed him the treasures there. Then they took him into the gardens and showed him the trees and flowers. Days went by, weeks went by, he almost lost track of time, but judging from the changing seasons, a year had passed. The old woman confirmed that he had been there a year and a day. The old man returned from time to time.

Einion was happy, contented and well-fed. He started to grow out of his clothes. But new ones appeared out of nowhere. After a while he began to miss his home and his family, especially his grandma. He wanted to tell her the story of his adventures.

Next time the old man appeared, he asked if he might leave the palace and return to his own world. The old man asked him to wait awhile.

After three days, one of the young women said that she was afraid that if he left he would never return and it would break her heart. He was thrilled to find that she loved him and he promised her that he would return. She gave him gifts and showed him the pathway home.

When he arrived his family were astounded. They had thought him dead. Indeed, another young shepherd had been accused of killing him and he had fled, apparently running away to America, but that's another story. Einion was pleased to see his family and be home again. He went back to his work as a shepherd.

One evening he was returning from a long day when three ewes had given birth. One had produced twins, and he had spent time encouraging the ewe, who was a little reluctant, to nurture both lambs.

He was exhausted, and he had an aching longing for the young woman who had asked him to promise to return.

When he arrived at home he told his family of his intention. Only his grandma understood. She persuaded the rest of the family to be pleased that he had found love.

He made his way to the standing stone. He tapped three times, just as he had seen the old man do. He put his arms around the enormous stone and found that it was light enough for him to easily lift it. He made his way down the winding steps, along the tunnel and through the woodland to the palace. There was the beautiful woman waiting for him, as if he was expected. He felt so much love for her that he immediately proposed marriage. She accepted. In an instant, the old man, the old woman and the two sisters gathered around them. Einion and the young woman made promises to each other and were pronounced husband and wife.

After much celebration which went on for days and days, Einion asked the young woman to come with him to his world, to meet his family and to live there with him. She agreed and accompanied him to his home where his family and particularly his grandma were thrilled to meet his new wife. His grandma gave the wife her own wedding ring, given to her when she was married many years before.

After a while a little boy was born to them. Friends and relatives came to greet the baby and to meet Einion's wife. It is true to say that they lived happily ever after.

I enjoyed this story very much and told my friend that I liked stories which ended with 'they all lived happily ever after'. 'So do I,' he said, 'but we must be careful to preserve all the stories, not just the happy ones.'

The following day we would continue our stories of the Preselis and would meet by the school in Cwm Gwaun.

As we departed, I looked at him out of the corner of my eye and said, very quickly so that I could sneak up on him, 'Rumpelstiltskin'.

He laughed and said, 'You will have to try harder than that.' I was pleased to have caused him some amusement. He often looked troubled and seemed weighed down with the burden of the quest. When he laughed his whole demeanour changed, the sound of his laughter was infectious. 'And just turn up – you've nothing to bring tomorrow,' he said as he disappeared behind the plaque.

# CWM GWAUN, GWAUN VALLEY

We met at the school in Cwm Gwaun, a place that plays a big part in keeping this valley special. My companion was at the gates, a large brown paper parcel under his left arm. We set off walking along the lane through the valley. As we walked, I told my companion all that I had learnt about this area, known for the Hen Galan festival, celebrating the New Year on 12 January.

Hen Galan, or old New Year, is based on the ancient Julian calendar which was superseded in the eighteenth century throughout Britain by the Gregorian calendar.

However, the people of the Gwaun Valley ignored this decree and carried on with the old ways. So every 12 January children continue to walk around the Gwaun Valley to receive their *calennig*, or gifts of sweets, fruit and money. They form groups and go from house to house, bearing good wishes for the health and prosperity of the household during the year to come. This is symbolised by skewered apples, and more recently an orange, stuck with cloves, corn and sprigs of evergreen, which they carry in their hands.

At each door they sing a song:

Mi godais heddiw ma's o'm tŷ
A'm cwd a'm pastwn gyda mi,
A dyma'm neges ar eich traws,
Sef llanw'm cwd â bara a chaws.

I left my house today
With my bag and my stick,
And here is my message to you,
Fill my bag with bread and cheese.

Often the *calennig* is made with a tripod of twigs and an orange or apple and displayed in the homes here in Cwm Gwaun.

My companion nodded wisely at my description of the *calennig*. Just then we passed the famous Dyffryn Arms, where the bar is the front room of Bessie Davies' house and the beer is served through a hatch straight from the barrel. Bessie has run the pub for over forty years and it has played an essential role in keeping Yr Hen Galan alive in the twenty-first century. My companion asked me to wait while he went round the back of the Dyffryn Arms. I noticed he returned without the parcel.

Then my companion asked me if I had heard of other traditions kept alive in this valley. I knew two others.

## Mari Lwyd

Another local tradition is the Mari Lwyd. The skull of a horse is attached to a pole so that the jaws can be snapped open and shut by the bearer, who is covered by a white sheet draped from the skull. The head is decorated with coloured ribbons, bells and flowers. Local people join the procession and call at local houses. The Mari Lwyd would challenge the householders to join the singing and recitation of verses. If the Mari could 'subdue the inmates with superior witticisms and extempore humorous rhymes' (if the householder cannot respond with a verse or song), the party must be invited inside to partake of good cheer.

The thought crossed my mind that the parcel my friend had left behind at the pub was about the size and shape of a horse's head.

## Noson Gyflaith (Toffee Evening)

This is another traditional event at this time of year. Everyone had a hand in the pulling process once the ingredients were brought to exactly the right temperature and consistency. The hot toffee was poured onto a slate slab and the pulling began when members of the family and friends were gathered. A lot of talking and laughing weas the most successful result, especially if the toffee never hardened.

My companion nodded and smiled when I told him. He said he was pleased that the old celebrations were still taking place. He knew Bessie and often blessed the ale she served.

I looked at him and asked if his name was 'Ffynnon Gwynt' (meaning Wind Well, since both had featured in some of our tales and indeed in all stories ever since the first tales were told). He looked at me again and said, 'Not bad, but wrong.' He paused, and then added, 'So you're interested in wells?' I nodded eagerly. 'Good. I have a story about Brynberian. If you want to hear it, we should meet there tomorrow at the usual time.'

# BRYNBERIAN

The meeting place was on the bridge which crossed Afon Brynberian. A friend of mine was house-sitting here while the owners were abroad. I left my car parked outside, and had coffee with her before joining my companion. He was already waiting for me by the bridge.

He said that this was a very special place and related a story.

## THE LEGEND OF THE AFANC

The Afanc was a gigantic and fearful creature living on the Preseli slopes somewhere above the village of Brynberian. It ravaged the countryside, killing livestock and ruining the crops. The Afanc's birthplace was underwater, where it was born out of the very clay of a deep pool by the bridge in Brynberian. With the body of a beaver and the head of a crocodile, it was said that only magic would defeat the Afanc.

The inhabitants of Brynberian, living in daily fear for their lives, consulted the Dyn Hysbys – the wisest of folk – for guidance on ridding themselves of the monster that created so much chaos.

They were advised to slay him by magic. But the villagers did not know any suitable magic, so, meeting together, they agreed an alternative plan: a trick. They delegated a group of people to ask him to dig a well for the village.

He laughed and threw stones at them. They tried a second time, bringing a newly baked cake. The Afanc swallowed the cake in one mouthful, fell asleep, and started to snore. So they came a third time, bringing a bowl of cawl. He slurped down all the soup, and then eyed this group of people. After a dreadful pause, he told them that he would dig the well for them if they promised to bring him cake and soup every day for the rest of his life.

The villagers looked at each other and nodded. Their spokesman said that they agreed his terms (if their plan worked there would not be too many days more to bring cake and soup). He then agreed to do the work and immediately started digging furiously.

As the excavation steadily deepened, the villagers looked down, waiting until he had dug to a great depth ('over one hundred yards' was recorded). Then they tipped huge white stones into the hole, intending to crush him to death. Well satisfied, they all went home and back to bed.

But next morning they found the Afanc still digging. He said that there had been a rather heavy snowstorm on the previous day.

They tried many other tricks, but all of them failed. The Afanc continued killing livestock and spoiling crops for decades, as generations of villagers passed on. Years later the Afanc finally met its end, reportedly 'dying a natural death.'

The Afanc was buried on the hillside outside Brynberian. His tomb is a cairn of stones. You can see for yourself – follow any map to Bedd yr Afanc, out on the Preseli moors.

Sometime after I heard this story from my companion, I found the essay on 'North Pembrokeshire Folklore' by T.R. Davis, a former schoolmaster of Newport School. He heard this same story from shepherds and farmers in the Preseli district.

Before we parted I had another guess at his name: 'Sam Evans', since they were both names which had appeared in our adventures so far.

He shook his head. 'You can surely do better than that.'
I felt I was getting nowhere, so changed the subject. 'Are all our meeting places significant?' My brain was whirring; many of our meetings were beside bridges, so perhaps his name reflected this.

I ventured another guess: 'Pont?' This means bridge in both Welsh and French. He smiled but shook his head and said meeting by a bridge was bound to happen frequently in this county which was criss-crossed by so many rivers and streams.

'Concentrate on the stories,' he said.

# TREFDRAETH, NEWPORT

The next day we met by the Memorial Hall in Newport. I had seen some good performances in this hall, and wanted to tell my friend about some of them – classical music, Indian music, drama – the list was long. For the first time I wanted to tell my companion a bit more about my own life and interests.

But he was having none of it. He simply interrupted me, saying there were people in this town who were good at predicting the future. He was hoping to meet one of them here.

At least he noticed that I was a bit put out at being interrupted, so to make amends he volunteered a story.

# BUTTER MAKER

There was a woman in the 1920s who was a proficient butter maker. She often taught young women, for it was mostly women who performed this art. She shared her skills and offered tips which were particularly useful when the butter wouldn't 'come'.

But on one occasion, rather than being grateful to the butter maker, a younger woman, called Sara, was angry. She felt that the older woman had made her look a fool. In no time at all, after the butter maker took over the churning, the butter was perfect. Unlike others who had been helped or instructed, Sara refused to give a token of thanks. She was suspicious that the butter maker was procuring the gratitude of her novices, and their gifts, by putting a hex on the butter in the first place to prevent it turning.

In the hearing of others, Sara accused the older woman of mischief. The butter maker laughed, looked at her accuser, and said that it was her slack churning that was at fault.

Sara was angry at this, and told many in the village that much damage had been done, not only to butter but to cattle and crops, by local 'witches'.

However, the rest of the village knew the older butter maker as a kindly soul and so these accusations foundered.

I was still put out by my companion ignoring what I wanted to say about Trefdraeth, so I risked criticising his tale: 'That's about a mischievous claim of witchcraft. It's not about predicting the future at all. But in any case, I knew the butter story already – it's from the work of Bertram Lloyd. And as it happens he has collected tales of premonitions of death. Do you want to hear some?'

I knew I'd overstepped the mark, but my companion appeared not to notice and asked to hear my stories.

## SOUNDS IN THE NIGHT

There was a woman who lived in a house just behind the Parrog in Trefdraeth. The Parrog is a name given to streets or settlements in this part of Pembrokeshire that stand directly on the seashore. The woman's husband was working away from home, so she lived mostly alone. One night she woke up to hear noises downstairs coming from the kitchen. Furniture was being pushed around and heavy objects were falling to the floor. She was much afraid and took a candle and went downstairs to investigate. Everything was in its place and there was no sign of anything having been moved. Perhaps it might be rats, or a neighbour's cat had got into the house.

She searched the pantry and the cupboards, but found nothing and no signs of disturbance, so went back to bed. As soon as she laid her head on the pillow, the noises started all over again. Now she was really scared and would have climbed out of her bedroom window if it hadn't been so high. She hid under the bedclothes till morning.

The next day she told her neighbour, who was very sympathetic and volunteered to stay the night with her. No noises were heard.

Several weeks later her husband returned home from working away. He was very ill. His wife put him to bed and looked after him. Two days later he died.

When the undertakers came, they found it necessary to move much furniture around to make way for the coffin. In doing so, they dislodged various heavy articles which fell thudding to the floor. The widow, laying out her husband ready for his funeral, heard the noises downstairs and recognised them as the succession of noises she had heard a few nights earlier.

## Baying at the Moon

Barking dogs are linked to superstitions about the portent of death. There is a tale from Trefdraeth about a woman who lived on the Parrog, close to the beach. One night, she heard a dog endlessly baying or 'barking with a cold sound', as she described it. The animal was outside a particular house and couldn't be moved. Neighbours came and threw buckets of water over the dog, but it made no difference.

There was a local belief that death was foretold in the household at which a dog was barking. The woman reporting the barking was glad it wasn't outside her house. She was relieved that she lived near the sea. It was difficult for a dog to bark outside when the tide was in. Another Parrog-dweller reported that she couldn't sleep when she heard a dog howling 'in that cold way'. It made her worry about who was going to be 'for it'.

I told my companion that when I first visited Pembrokeshire, I had come to this beautiful bay. The pictures of seascapes in my childhood picture books had looked just like this.

Tomorrow we were to meet in Dinas, along the coast from Trefdraeth. I told him about some friends who lived there, well-known gardeners and bee-keepers, although like all bee-keepers they faced increasing threats to the health of their hives. He said I should tell them that it would get better, but they would need patience. I said that all gardeners were blessed with patience, otherwise we wouldn't sow and plant year after year and put up with the pests and diseases. He told me that if I wanted one plant, I should plant six seeds: one for the mice, one for the birds, one for snails, one for slugs, one for rabbits and one for myself. I smiled.

# DINAS

We met by the chip shop. My friend was already sitting on the bench outside. I went in and bought us a cup of tea and local Welsh cakes. He enjoyed them so much that he launched straight into a story.

## HEART DOCTOR

In Dinas, stories are told of Daniel Thomas, who lost a number of his cows and calves. His wife's cousin, Edwin Lewis in Gelli, near Cilgwyn, was also losing his cattle mysteriously. They had both observed calves running around on their knees in the byre, obviously in agony. Several fat sows had been observed jumping high in the air before they died.

Thomas and Lewis could not explain these strange deaths, so they agreed to consult the well-known local wise man 'Dr' Harries. He listened to their story and told them to cut out the heart of the most recently dead beast on Lewis' farm; and then to take the heart, whilst not uttering a word to anyone, stick it full of pine needles, take it into Lewis' kitchen and burn it over the kitchen fire.

They carefully carried out these instructions. The animal's heart was hung on the big hook on the end of a chain over the open hearth. They locked the door and they waited, sitting in the simne fawr (inglenook), taking care not to utter a word.

Whilst the heart slowly burned, the farmhouse door rattled and was beaten upon. Excited voices cried out, 'Let us in, let us in'. The farmers steeled themselves and took no notice and still spoke not a word. The voices then started to wail and howl in agony. Lewis said that this made him feel physically sick. After the heart was burnt, the two men went outside and found that the voices belonged to Thomas' two sisters. They were jealous that Thomas' new wife, Mary, was now living on the farm. Until his marriage, it had been their home. They had been responsible for the killings, the spoilt crops and the chaos. They had included Lewis in their campaign because he was Thomas' friend and cousin to the new wife.

The burning of the heart was said to have dispelled their witchcraft.

Conjurors were often given the title 'Doctor'. Their powers were employed in many ways from major problems to the finding of lost articles.

'It is a pity we can't get one of these wise people to find the objects on your list,' I said.

My companion disagreed. 'You can never be sure whether or not mischief is being made, or an obstacle is being placed in your path.' He added he would rather carry on with my help. I was touched and felt a warm inner glow.

# ABERGWAUN, FISHGUARD

The next day we were to meet by the standing stones in Lota Park, a lovely green area given to the town by Walter Williams, the son of a local sea captain, William Williams. It is named after the town of Lota in Chile, where Walter was born during one of Williams' long voyages overseas.

As I waited I recalled another local man who told stories.

## TOM FURLONG

Tom lived alone in a wooden hut on the cliff side behind Main Street. It was a humble dwelling but served him well. As a young man he worked in the family's coaching business. His father ran the early mail coach service.

When he was older he seemed to live by his wits, with no visible means of support. He was a well-known local character, a great raconteur, but his sense of humour often got him into trouble. The young men of the town played practical jokes, which he regarded as a challenge and often got his own back threefold.

Tom's friends often visited his windswept shack regularly just to listen to his yarns. He told his stories with such animation and with many gesticulations. His friends were always highly entertained. A visit to Tom Furlong's was better than going to the cinema and all they had to bring to Tom's hut was a jug or bottle of ale and something for the table in the 'pot luck' tradition of Pembrokeshire.

Although a bachelor, Tom assured the assembled company that he often had his moments. There was one time when a newspaper sales representative came to his door. He 'gave her a nice cup of tea in a nice clean cup' and they got chatting, after which he offered her a bed for the night which, to his surprise, she accepted. But the romantic evening was ruined because some of Tom's young friends threw a big boulder down onto the zinc roof of the shack just as the couple were going to bed. The loud rumblings on the roof dampened Tom's ardour. He later wrote in a lady's journal that: 'I was so frightened I was flummoxed for the rest of the night.' His language was rather more colourful when he described the incident to his friends.

Despite his peculiar lifestyle and fun-loving demeanour, Tom Furlong was very interested in his local community and supportive of people's welfare. He was a prolific letter writer and full of ideas for potential profitable developments for Fishguard and Goodwick. He often wrote to government ministers, industrialists and potential investors, making all sorts of suggestions. No one heard of any of the ideas coming to fruition but he was never put off. 'Well,' he would laugh, 'it only cost a three ha'penny stamp anyway.'

Lost in remembering the story, I had closed my eyes and nodded off. Suddenly I was awoken by loud throat clearing. It was my companion, clearly impatient and worried.

I asked him if he had known Tom Furlong. He said that he did, and that Tom kept many stories alive by retelling them.

# WDIG, GOODWICK

We were still short of a mermaid hair or two, and I remembered a tale of a mermaid sighting near Goodwick. So I suggested walking to Fishguard's twin town, just a mile or two away. On the way I told my companion about a farmer on Pencaer, the peninsula beyond Goodwick. One day the farmer went out to close his chickens in for the night, when he found a mermaid sitting on a rock near his farm. He captured her, and put her in a sack. She pleaded with him to set her free, but instead he took her back to the farmhouse. She was unhappy and became very ill.

Eventually she died, but as she drew her last breath, she put a curse on the farm, that no children would be born there. And for centuries there was not the cry of a baby to interrupt the long winter nights on that farm.

I gather that some years ago a new owner placated the *Plant Rhys Dwfn*, by giving them food, warmth and kindness. Leaving the fire alight and bread and milk on the kitchen table at night eventually served as an apology. The curse has now, apparently, been lifted.

At Goodwick we walked slowly up steep Stop and Call Hill. 'Do you know how it got this name?' my friend asked.

'Is it because many years ago when the mail coach came up this hill out of Goodwick they had to stop and call at the top?' I asked. My friend was unconvinced.

'That doesn't explain another house further along here called Pass-by. It's on all the old maps,' he said.

'Please tell me, then,' I said.

My friend looked mischievous. 'You're meant to be the storyteller –' Before he could tell me off any more, we were halted by the sight of a collection of American cars. My companion, surprisingly, seemed very interested in the cars, and spent some time looking round them. He even stood on a handy ramp to peer through the windows.

I persuaded him to continue walking to the farm where the mermaid had been captured. It was many years ago, but it seems that mermaid hairs will often remain at the scene of an encounter with humans. We searched along the lane and along the coastal path. We looked high up in the thorny branches of hawthorns, and deep in the mouths of badger setts, but with no luck. It was not a good day, and my companion looked downhearted.

To lighten the mood a little I asked him if he had heard of a local storyteller called Shcmi Wad (Jamie Wade). He said he certainly had and that this storyteller had been a favourite locally. (His stories have been collected by Mary Medlicott in her book which bears his name).

The following day we would meet at Abercastle and I was to bring a loaf of bread. Not just any old loaf of bread, of course, but one I baked myself from spelt flour and decorated with sunflower seeds.

I stayed up late to mix bread dough. Easy for me, since I always bake my own bread and I happened to have a sack of spelt flour and a jar of sunflower seeds. I left the dough proving whilst I slept, and baked two loaves in the morning, just to be on the safe side.

# ABERCASTLE

When I arrived in Abercastle the bread was still warm. My companion was delighted to see not one, but two loaves. Sitting on the harbour wall looking out of the narrow bay to sea, we ate one loaf just as it was – no butter or cheese, just good fresh warm bread. As we ate, a triple-masted tall ship sailed past on the horizon. I was thrilled to see this reminder of bygone times. My friend seemed unsurprised, as if he had been expecting it. He told me a story about this tiny fishing harbour.

## IWAN LLEWELLYN

Despite their bad reputation, the *Tylwyth Teg* are sometimes known for their kindness. People would often leave out a bath filled with water, a jug of milk or some newly baked bread for them. It was understood that these small people preferred to confer their good magic on a household which is kept clean and tidy.

Iwan Llewellyn lived in a small tidy cottage overlooking the harbour in Abercastle. He would often leave a fire burning in the grate, to keep the *Tylwyth Teg* warm on a winter night. He knew they frequently visited because he could hear them in his kitchen when he was in bed.

One starry night he was awake and he heard them enter the kitchen, moving around and talking in low voices. He strained his ears to hear what was being said. One voice was louder than the rest and Iwan heard the words quite distinctly. 'It's cold tonight. I wish we could have some cheese and bread, but this poor man has only a morsel left, plenty for us but he might starve without it.'

Iwan cried out, telling them to take whatever they wanted, then turned over to sleep.

In the morning he went into the kitchen, to see if the fairies had left him any scraps of food. When he opened the cupboard door he was astonished to see a great wedge of good Welsh cheese and a loaf of freshly baked bread.

Iwan went to the door of his cottage, turned to face inland towards the Allt (a steep wooded valley) where everyone knew the fairies lived, and shouted out to them. He thanked them, wished them good luck, and the good fortune never to go hungry. As he walked back into his kitchen he saw a shilling on the corner of the dresser. Every morning after that he woke up to find a loaf of bread, a wedge of cheese and a shilling on the corner of the dresser.

His neighbours called him lucky Iwan for he was wealthy and had plenty to eat, without ever seeming to do any work.

He married a widow, and they were happy together until she became curious about his wealth. Every morning she saw a new shilling on the dresser, and eventually her curiosity got the better of her. She asked Iwan, but he refused to tell her. She insisted, saying it wasn't fair for him to keep secrets from her. After all, they were married – partners in life – and she had a right to know. Again and again she asked. Iwan became angry. To silence her, he warned that if he ever told her about the good luck, it would stop. There would be no more money.

Now she understood that it was fairy money. She asked him directly – was it the fairies? He then had to admit that it was so. And as soon as he made the admission, the five shillings in his pocket turned to stones. No more money was left on the corner of the dresser, and no more bread and cheese was left in the cupboard.

After that Iwan Llewellyn had to go out to find work. But in truth it was the best thing that ever happened to him. He even found that his wife baked a fine loaf. Having learnt his lesson, he forgave her curiosity, never kept any more secrets from her, and they lived a long and happy life together.

Since we had no luck the previous day in finding the remaining mermaid hairs on Pencaer, I suggested Trefin as our next port of call.

# TREFIN

We met the next day at Trefin and I told the story that I had heard about a mermaid here.

## MEDI YN SIR BENFRO – REAPING IN PEMBROKESHIRE

There were once some quarrymen working in Porth y Rhaw quarry. They enjoyed working here on a clear day like this. The sun was warm and there was enough of a sea breeze to refresh them. The flowers near the quarry smelled sweet. The jagged rocks served as a wind-break when the storms blew up. Just occasionally a wave rose up and struck the rugged cliffs, but the sea, often wild and stormy, was today as smooth and calm as a mirror.

As the men took their break to eat their food and drink some ale, they looked across the calm blue sea and were distracted by a man running along the path which led from Fishguard to St Davids. They called to him and he arrived panting and in quite a lather. They bade him sit and join them but he was too distracted. They offered him some ale which he drank down to the last drop. When he finally calmed down, he sat and introduced himself as Daniel Huws. He explained that he was on the coast path near Trefin when he saw one of the ladies of *Rhys Ddwfn*. She was sitting on top of a boulder to disentangle her flowing greenish-silvery hair.

The quarrymen were keen to see this maiden and Daniel Huws led them to the place. They saw that she still sat on the rock, and they hid close by to watch her. It was quite clear that from her waist upwards, she was just like the lasses of Wales, but that from her waist downwards, she had the body of a fish.

They called to her, being careful to keep their distance and their voices gentle, lest they scare her away. They found she spoke Welsh, although she only uttered the following few words to them: 'Medi yn Sir Benfro, Chwynnu yn Sir Gâr' (Reaping in Pembrokeshire and weeding in Carmarthenshire.) She then slipped down from the rock and slid into the sea towards home.

The men looked at each other in surprise and delight, not only to have seen but to have conversed with a mermaid. But none of them could make sense of her words. As far as they could tell, the mermaid's message was good news for Pembrokeshire – reaping

the harvest is better than pulling weeds. But was that really what she meant? When they arrived home and told their wives, the ale was blamed and the women who brewed the ale in their village were asked to water down the beer in future for their men's lunch.

The man had listened carefully to my tale, and without a word, led us off to a high point on the coast path, where a large boulder overlooked the sea. We searched around the rock, and in the lush undergrowth at its foot. Sure enough we found another hair, long and curled, with the same silvery greenish hue as the first hair. My companion inspected it and declared that it would do. There was the glimmer of a triumphant smile as he wrapped it separately, and put a second tissue-wrapped parcel in his hat.

Before going home I went to look at the ruined corn mill on the very edge of the sea at Aberfelin. When I reached home I hunted out the famous poem of Archdruid Crwys 'Melin Trefin'. The mill had ground corn for around 500 years and was used by the villagers of Trefin and the surrounding areas. Wheat was milled to produce flour for bread baking, and barley was ground into winter feed for livestock.

### Melin Trefin

Nid yw'r felin heno'n malu
Yn Nhrefin ym min y mor,
Trodd y merlyn olaf adre' …

Tonight the mill no longer grinds
In Trefin, close by the sea
For the last time, the pony has turned for home …

The next day we were to meet at St David's, but not at the cathedral, nor even at the Bishop's Palace. We were to meet, once again, on a bridge. This one was below the cathedral fields, over a fast–moving stream. The rushing water made me think about the breathless pace of our journey. And looking over the fields to the ancient cathedral in this tiny city, I realised how typical of Pembrokeshire it was to have such an important building and community in such a small place. It seemed to embody Dewi's own motto: Remember the small things.

This time I had brought with me a copy of *Madoc*, by the romantic poet Robert Southey, to read to my friend when he appeared.

It was a windy day and I searched in my rucksack for a hat to keep my hair in order. Then I blinked: once again my friend had appeared as if out of nowhere. I had never seen him arrive at or leave any of our meeting places.

# Tyddewi, St David's

### *Gavran*

Where are the sons of Gavran? where his tribe
The faithful? Following their beloved Chief,
They the Green Islands of the Ocean sought;
Nor human tongue hath told, nor human ear,
Since from the silver shores they went their way,
Hath heard their fortunes. In his crystal Ark,
Whither sail'd Merlin with his band of Bards,
Old Merlin, master of the mystic lore?

Twice have the sons of Britain left her shores,
As the fledged eaglets quit their native nest;
Twice over ocean have her fearless sons
For ever sail'd away.

Robert Southey

My friend told me that this was the tale of the twelfth-century Welsh Prince who set sail westwards and discovered America, no less. And the green islands of the poem are those off the coast at St Davids: Ramsey; The Bishops and Clerks (a reef of tiny islets and rocks, individually named: Maen Rhoson; Carreg Rhoson; North Bishop; Daufraich; Maen Daufraich; Cribog; Moelyn; Llechau Isaf; Llech Uchaf; Em-sger or South Bishop; Carreg Trai; and Gwahan); Pont Ynys-Bery; Ynys Eilun; Pont yr Eilan; Ynys Cantwr; Midland; and many more. Each name conceals a story.

These islands, called by Southey 'Green Spots of the Floods' are surrounded by the sea, and by many superstitions.

Like the occasionally visible land off Pen Cemaes, they are said to be the home of the *Tylwyth Teg*, or the fairy family – the souls of the virtuous Druids. They had a love of mischief, sometimes sad, and sometimes happy. They would visit the earth, seize a man, and demand to know if he would travel above wind, mid-wind, or below wind.

Above wind is a giddy, whirling and terrible passage, below wind is through thorns, bushes and rocks. Be warned that the middle is not a safe course. In order to safeguard yourself you must catch hold of the grass, for it is well known that these spirits do not have the power to destroy a blade of grass.

There are times when these spirits are in better moods, and they come over and carry the Welsh in their boats to their islands. He who visits these islands imagines upon his return that he has been absent only a few hours, when, in truth, whole centuries have passed by.

The story fascinated me, and I told my friend that I had heard that if you take turf from St David's churchyard, and stand upon it on the seashore, you behold these islands. One man, who did this, immediately put to sea to find them. But the islands disappeared, and his search was in vain.

He returned to land, looked at them again from the enchanted turf, once again set sail, and failed again. The third time he brought the turf into his vessel, and stood upon it till he succeeded in reaching them.

My friend agreed that the very turf of St David's was alive with legends. He told me another.

## St David

Almost 2,000 years ago, a young man called Sant was visited by a spirit who told him to keep a piece of land for thirty years in readiness for a son who would be born to him. He kept the land despite many temptations to sell it, particularly as he had not married.

The same spirit visited St Patrick and advised him not to settle in Pembrokeshire as this was reserved for a boy who would be born thirty years later. Patrick was rather put out but followed the instruction, since he was told that it was his life task to look after the whole of Ireland.

Sant became enamoured of a young woman called Non and he seduced her, perhaps against her will. Some months later whilst thunder roared and lightning crashed, she gave birth, in a stone circle, close to what is now St Non's Chapel. Within the stone circle there was no storm, all was calm and quiet, the sun shone warmly on the grass and on the young woman as she gave birth. The child was named Dewi (David). After she gave birth a spring of pure, clear water came out of the ground.

I realised that in the same book I had brought with the Southey poem was a poem by another English poet, Michael Drayton, about Dewi and his connection with water. I found the page and read it to my friend:

> As he did only drink what crystal Hodney yields,
> And fed upon the leeks he gathered in the fields
> In memory of whom, in each revolving year,
> The Welshmen, on his day, that sacred herb do wear.

I explained to my friend that it was St David's spirit who convinced the Welsh to wear a leek, so that they could be distinguished in battle, as well as to celebrate St David's Day on 1 March.

My companion was amused, and said that before every feast day there was a night of trouble, such as St David's Eve for example.

## CWN ANNWN

February 28th is St David's Eve and one of the favoured nights for the Cwn Annwn (hounds of Annwn, the underworld) to take to the skies. They race and howl across the land, the souls of the damned and they hunt for more souls to feed the furnaces of hell. Sometimes they are seen as huge dogs with human heads.

'There's another date connected with Dewi,' I said, and told my friend about Old St David's Day (March 12th) when the wax candle on the table was replaced by a wooden one, signifying that supper could be eaten without candlelight – the end of the winter months.

My companion smiled: 'Are you starting to read my thoughts?' he asked. Then he explained why: the following day he needed a candlestick.

Because I was unsure about all this travelling, I asked if he might prefer to give me a list and I would find the things. He could snuggle up beside a cosy fire at my home and I would give him the collection once it was assembled.

He explained to me that the time and place of handover or finding of the objects were as important as the items. Also hadn't he made it clear that all the objects had come from his own world and he'd been told to take them back there?

I just couldn't see how my mother's ring, the old woman's key and the candlestick could possibly have come from his world. Then the thought dawned on me that these familiar objects had all been found at one time or other. They all had a previous existence.

There was indeed an old enamel candle holder at home, which I often took along as inspiration for stories at writing workshops. When I described it he agreed that it was worth a try, and that I should bring it the next day, when we should meet at Cantre'r Gwaelod.

'That's just not possible! The nearest we can get is Ramsey Island.' He looked angry and upset, so I explained how Cantre'r Gwaelod was deep beneath the sea. Begrudgingly he conceded. Ramsey would have to do.

I asked him if his name was David or Dai or Dewi. He shook his head and frowned. He muttered something about 'call yourself a storyteller?' under his breath as he walked away.

Something else was bothering me. On each of our excursions he appeared as if from nowhere. He didn't travel with me in my small red car, even though I had offered to pick him up on a few occasions. He had always given me a quizzical look and said that he would meet me there. This time I was determined to watch him and see where and how he went.

Unfortunately the wind blew my scarf from around my neck. By the time I had retrieved it he had gone. It reminded me of the first time I'd seen him, when the wind blew some grit in my eye. Hmm!

The next day I took the boat from St Justinian's to Ramsey Island. I half-expected to meet my companion aboard, but apart from an elderly couple come to scatter the ashes of a friend, and a company of scouts, there was no one else on the little boat. It was quite rough and I felt a little queasy when I reached the island.

I sat for a while to regain my composure, closing my eyes, which did nothing to prevent the nausea. When I opened them he was there. He handed me a bunch of herbs and told me to sniff them. I did and felt immediately better. He spotted the candle holder and asked where it had come from. 'It was in the house when I moved in; the previous owner had left it in a barn.' I had found it covered in dust and grime, and a varied selection of mouse droppings and cobwebs. After time spent cleaning it, I was pleased that it was undamaged – a nice bright-green enamel, with a curved handle. It was very practical and was particularly useful during a power cut. Ordinary household candles fitted perfectly.

I had left a candle in it, in case it was no good without. I was trying really hard to get things right, because my companion was very particular. He looked at it again and smiled, as if he was greeting an old friend. He even thanked me. Things were looking up.

I asked if his name was Jack, remembering the nursery rhyme: 'Jack be nimble, Jack be quick, Jack jump over the candle stick.'

It was, of course, wrong, but he was clearly amused.

# THE ISLANDS OF RAMSEY AND BARDSEY

Cantre'r Gwaelod, also known as Cantref Gwaelod or Cantref y Gwaelod (The Lowland Hundred), is a legendary ancient sunken kingdom, a tract of fertile land lying between Ramsey Island and Bardsey Island. It has been described as a 'Welsh Atlantis' and is remembered in folklore, literature and song.

Where is it? Somewhere under the waters of Cardigan Bay, some twenty miles out from the present coast. Welsh literature and legend has never forgotten its lost hundred.

We sat on rocks looking out from Ramsey into the Atlantic, where Madoc had disappeared nine centuries earlier. Far below us on the shingle beach of Porth Lleuog, at least sixteen seals were resting in the sunshine. For the first time in this breathless journey, we also both relaxed a little. Soon my companion stirred and offered an island story.

## MERERID

Mererid was a well-maiden. She had been sent to the well at Maes Gwyddno to clear the weeds from the springs which fed the well. As she bent over pulling at the duck weed, someone started to sing behind her and she jumped out of her skin. She looked round to see whose voice was making music. There stood a young man with dark curly hair and a charming smile. He offered to help her, but suggested that she should first share some wine from the flagon he had with him.

There was always plenty of water to refresh her as she worked at this well, but now she tasted the wine, and enjoyed it. She sat down, and the young man sang to her. His voice captivated her; it was like honey. His dark-green eyes twinkled. He made her laugh, and she forgot about the work she had been sent to do. When he kissed her she melted into his arms.

They spent some time at the well, hardly noticing when their feet became wet, followed by their ankles, legs, and bodies. Suddenly realising what was happening, they ran from the flood, which continued to rise as they ran and ran. The land was lost to the floods and sank beneath the sea.

That young man, a Prince called Seithenyn, was the sluice-gate keeper at the place where the low lands of Cantre'r Gwaelod were defended from the sea by a dyke called Sarn Badrig (St Patrick's causeway). He was a notorious drunkard, and perhaps not the best person to be left in charge of the dyke. Whilst he dallied with Mererid, he had failed to close the floodgates. Through his negligence, the sea swept through the open sluice, engulfing the land.

The waves were booming in the sea caves far below us as my friend finished his tale. Sometimes people thought they heard bells in these waters. Indeed, the church bells of Cantre'r Gwaelod are said to ring out in times of danger. I have often listened out for them but I have never heard them. Please let me know if you do.

The next place was Narberth. 'What am I to bring this time?' I asked.

'Nothing at all, but you will have to help me find an entrance.'

I remembered the old woman I had met a few weeks ago, who had spoken of the three portals into the 'Otherworld'. Arberth (Narberth) was one of them. I became excited and started to form a question in my mind. 'Don't,' he warned, seeming to read my mind. 'Sometimes it's better not to know. I am happy to share stories with you, which I hope you will pass on to others, but I cannot tell you about the entrances.'

I felt privileged to be part of the journey and didn't ask more about tomorrow, even though my head was buzzing with them. This quest was exceeding all expectations, but concern about the time taken and my publisher's deadline was replaced by satisfaction as I returned home each night with a new set of tales for my book, and to tell to others orally. Thanks to my strange friend, I was relieved that I was still on schedule.

He accompanied me on the boat back to St Justinians. A flock of gannets followed us screeching and diving for food. I wanted to look around for signs of porpoises or dolphins in the water, but was feeling too queasy. I searched in my rucksack and found the bunch of herbs which I sniffed every time I felt sick. With relief I climbed onto the dock and turned round to offer a hand to my friend. He had gone. He never ceased to amaze me.

I was still nowhere near guessing his name either. I seemed to be failing him in that. I listed all the things we had gathered so far to see if they could point to a name or be amalgamated in some way.

Mermaid's hair ... key ... box ... ring ... candlestick ... Then there was the Draenog. What was that creature's role in this quest?

# ARBERTH, NARBERTH

It was a busy weekday when I met the man by the market cross in Narberth. He pointed the way to a mound just outside the small market town, now the site of Narberth Castle, ruined but well-kept and very magical. We quickly left the hubbub of the small town behind us as we walked to the spot. I was careful to remain standing, since the consequences of sitting on that mound have been well documented.

We searched and searched for something that would indicate an entrance but found nothing. My friend also looked for a note or clue to indicate that this may be the place, but without success. However my companion needed to be sure. Our search became wider and wider. As the light faded, we were still without whatever clue or message he was seeking. I suggested that we stop and continue tomorrow. He agreed to meet at the same place on the following day at midday.

Then he asked me to leave him, since he wished to sit on the mound to find out more. I couldn't help but start to question him, but he gave me a piercing look and shook his head. I apologised and left him there, sitting on the mound.

I worried all the way home and spent a sleepless night thinking about what might befall my companion.

The next day I came to the castle mound and found him still sitting there, with a satisfied look on his face. 'All the next stages in this quest are settled,' he announced. Then he asked me to sit with him and listen to an important story. 'And for once, you must make notes, to make sure that you can retell this important myth.'

I hesitated. 'Isn't that rather dangerous here?' I knew about the mound at Narberth.

The man insisted: 'Every story leads the listeners and the teller into danger. That's why we must hear the story out – to learn how danger is overcome.' Seeing that my companion was serious, I suggested that we sit on the remains of the castle wall. He joined me there.

'This tale is the mother and father of them all,' the man continued. 'In times past, when they heard this story, young apprentices were learning the craft of storytelling. As they listened to the Mabinogi, they themselves became part of the tradition.'

## PWYLL PRINCE OF DYFED

Pwyll Prince of Dyfed was lord of the seven Cantrefs (hundreds or regions) of Dyfed. In the north: Cemais, Pebidiog and Emlyn; in the south, Penfro; in between, Rhos, Daugleddau and Gwarthaf. And Narberth was the very centre of Dyfed, which later became Pembrokeshire. Narberth was where Pwyll had his chief palace.

One day Pwyll wished to go and hunt in Cwm Cych, the steep, deep forest valley dividing the cantrefs of Cemais from Emlyn, and which today divides Pembrokeshire from Carmarthenshire. That very night he left Narbeth and reached Llwyn Diarwyd, where he rested. He rose early the next day and reached Cwm Cych, where he set his hounds loose in the wood, sounded the horn, and began the chase. But as he followed the hunt deep into the forest, first he lost his companions, and then his dogs. As he strained to hear, he heard quite different hounds barking and approaching from the opposite direction.

Finally Pwyll broke out into a glade at the bottom of the Cwm, and his hounds rejoined him. At the same instant a stag burst into the far side of the glade, chased by strange hounds. As the stag reached the middle of the glade, those other hounds overtook it and brought it down. But he was distracted from the magnificent stag by the strange pack, the like of which he had never seen. Their hair was brilliant shining white, their ears were red; the dazzling whiteness of their bodies made the redness of their ears glisten all the more.

Pwyll approached these hounds, drove them away, and set his own dogs upon the stag. Immediately he saw a rider approaching on a large light-grey steed, a hunting horn round his neck, wearing grey woollen hunting garb. The horseman drew near and spoke: 'Chieftain,' said he, 'I know who you are, and I do not greet you.'

'Indeed,' said Pwyll, 'you may well have such status that entitles you not to greet me.'

'But it is not my dignity that prevents me; it is on account of your own ignorance and lack of courtesy. Greater discourtesy I never saw in man than to drive away the dogs that were already killing the stag and to set your own upon it. I declare to Heaven that I will dishonour you more than the value of a hundred stags.'

'Oh Chieftain,' Pwyll replied, 'I have done ill and wish to make amends, but I do not know who you are.'

'I am a crowned king in my land.'

'Lord,' said Pwyll, may your days prosper, and what is your land?'

'Annwfn,' he answered – the Deep Land, the netherworld. 'I am Arawn, a King of Annwfn.'

'Lord,' said Pwyll, 'how may I make amends?'

'You may as follows. There is a man whose lands are close to mine, who is ever warring against me. He is Hafgan, another King in Annwfn. Rid me of his oppression, which you can easily do, and you will gain my friendship.'

'Gladly will I do this,' said Pwyll. 'Show me how.'

'I will send you to Annwfn in my stead, and give you the most beautiful lady you ever beheld as your bed companion. I will put my appearance on you, so that no chamber lad, no officer, nor any other follower realise that it is not I. This shall continue for a year from tomorrow, when we meet again in this place.'

'Yes,' said Pwyll, 'but when I have been there for a year, how do I find him of whom you speak?'

'One year from tonight,' said Arawn, 'the time is set for us to meet at the Ford; you will be there in my likeness. You will deliver a single stroke, and he shall no longer live. But if he asks you to give him another blow, do not, however much he pleads. When I did so, he recovered to fight the next day, as strong as he was before.'

'Indeed,' said Pwyll, 'how shall I manage the affairs of my own kingdom?'

Arawn replied, 'I will cause that no one in all your lands, no man or woman, shall know that I am not you, for I will go there in your place.'

'Gladly then,' said Pwyll, 'I will set forward.'

'Your path shall be smooth, and nothing shall detain you until you reach my realm. I myself will be your guide!'

So Arawn led Pwyll through the gates into the netherworld until he reached the palace. 'Behold,' he said, 'enter the Court. When you observe the service that is performed there, you will learn the customs of the Court.'

So Pwyll went forward to the Court. He saw sleeping grooms, and halls, and chambers, and the most beautiful buildings ever seen. He went into the hall to disrobe, youths and pages coming to disrobe him, all saluting him as he entered. Two knights came and took his hunting dress from him, and clothed him in silk and gold. A feast was prepared, and he watched the household and the host enter, and with them entered the Queen, the most beautiful woman that he had ever beheld. She wore a yellow robe of shining satin. They washed and went to the table, and sat, the Queen upon one side of him, and one who seemed to be an Earl on the other side.

Pwyll spoke with the Queen. By her speech, she was a lady of the most attractive conversation and good humour that there ever was. They enjoyed meat and drink, songs and feasting. Of all Courts on earth, this was surely the best supplied with food and drink, golden vessels and royal jewels. And Pwyll was satisfied that she suspected nothing.

Then he made his way to the bedchamber, where the Queen awaited. He got into bed beside her, turned his back and went to sleep. It was not what she expected. The next day there was again tenderness and friendly conversation between them, and all the following days likewise to the end of the year. Whatever affection they shared during the day did not continue in the bedchamber. Every night he turned his back on her and went to sleep.

He spent the year hunting, in music making, feasting, entertainment and conversation, until the night that was fixed for the conflict. The night arrived, remembered even in the furthest part of this realm. He set off for the meeting, the nobles of the kingdom with him. When he came to the Ford, a knight spoke: 'Lords, listen well. This confrontation is between two kings and between them only. Each claims the land and territory of the other. All of you stand aside and leave the fight to be between them.'

Thus the two kings approached each other in the middle of the Ford, and engaged. At the first blow, Pwyll, in the place of Arawn, struck Hafgan on the centre of the boss of his shield. It was cloven in half, his armour was broken, and Hafgan was borne to the ground. The blow was deadly. 'Oh Chieftain,' said Hafgan, 'what right do you have to cause my death? I did not injure you in anything. Why would you slay me? Since you have started to slay me, complete the job.'

'Ah, Chieftain,' he replied, 'I might regret that. Say what you may, I will not do so.'

'My trusty Lords,' said Hafgan, 'take me from here. My death has come.'

'My nobles,' said he who appeared as Arawn, 'consider who should be my subjects.'

'Lord,' said the nobles, 'there is no king over the whole of Annwfn but you.'

'Yes,' he replied, 'he who comes humbly should be received graciously, but he who does not shall be compelled by the force of swords.'

He received the homage of the men and began to conquer the country. The next day by noon, the two kingdoms were in his power. Then Pwyll went to keep his tryst, and returned to Cwm Cych.

And when he arrived, the King of Annwfn was there to meet him. Each rejoiced to see the other. 'Indeed,' said Arawn, 'I thank you for your friendship to me. I have heard everything. When you return to your lands, you will see all that I have done for you.'

Then Arawn restored to Pwyll Prince of Dyfed his proper appearance, and also his own, and returned to the Court of Annwfn. He rejoiced when he saw his household, whom he had not seen so long; but they had not known of his absence, and wondered no more than usual at his coming. That day was spent in joy and merriment; and he sat and conversed with his wife and his nobles. They feasted, and when he and his Queen went to bed, he threw his arms about her and kissed her long and hard. He laughed and talked and then made love with her. She looked at him in disbelief and asked him what had changed. She explained that she felt very hurt that he had turned his back on her and refused even to speak to her in the bedchamber for a whole year. He shouted out that he had a dear friend indeed! He then told his wife what had happened. She was surprised and agreed that Pwyll was a good friend.

Pwyll Prince of Dyfed came to his lands, and asked his nobles how his rule had been in the past year, compared with previously. 'Lord,' said they, 'your wisdom was never so great, and you were never so kind or so free in bestowing thy gifts. Your justice was never more worthily seen than this year.'

'You should thank him who has been with you for all the good you have enjoyed.'

Pwyll related the whole story. 'Indeed, Lord,' said they, 'will you continue the rule which we have enjoyed for this past year?' Pwyll answered that he would.

Pwyll and Arawn forged a strong alliance. They sent each other horses, greyhounds, hawks and jewels to please the other. Spending that year in Annwfn, ruling there so prosperously, and uniting the two warring kingdoms in one day, he lost the name Pwyll Prince of Dyfed, and henceforward was called Pwyll Pen Annwfn – Pwyll Head of Annwfn.

Sometime later Pwyll rested at Narberth, his chief palace. A feast was prepared for him, and many of his men joined him. After the first meal, Pwyll set off to walk to the mound above the palace, Gorsedd Arberth. 'Lord,' warned one of the Court, 'the mound is remarkable. Whoever sits on it cannot leave without either receiving wounds or blows, or else seeing a wonder.'

'I am not afraid to receive wounds and blows. But as to the wonder, I would gladly see it. I will go and sit upon the mound.'

And as he sat upon the mound, a lady on a large pure white horse, with a garment of shining gold around her, came along the road. The horse seemed to move at a slow, steady pace, and to be coming up towards the mound. Pwyll asked his men, 'Is there any among you who knows that lady?' There was not.

'Go one of you and meet her, so that we may know who she is.' One of the men went to the road to meet her, but she passed by. He followed as fast as he could, but the faster he went, the further she was from him. When he saw that it was pointless to follow her, he returned to Pwyll: 'Lord, it is idle for anyone in the world to follow her on foot.'

'Go to the palace, take the fleetest horse and go after her,' Pwyll replied.

He took a horse and came to an open level plain, and spurred his horse. But the more he urged his horse, the further she was from him. Yet she held the same steady pace as before. He returned to Pwyll saying: 'Lord, it is pointless for anyone to follow that lady. There is no horse in the realm swifter than this, and I could not pursue her.'

'This must be some illusion.' said Pwyll. 'Let us return to the palace.'

The next day after the first meal, Pwyll said, 'The same party will go to the top of the mound. And you,' – he indicated one of his young men – 'take the swiftest horse you know.' So they went towards the mound, taking the horse with them. Once again they beheld the lady on the same horse, in the same apparel, coming along the same road.

'See the lady from yesterday,' said Pwyll. 'Get ready, youth, to learn who she is.'

'Gladly, lord,' said he. As the lady came past, the youth mounted his horse. Before he had settled in his saddle, she passed by, and there was a clear space between them. But her speed was no greater than it had been the day before. He put his horse into an amble, thinking that despite the gentle pace of his horse, he should soon overtake her. But she drew further away, so he gave his horse the reins. Still he came no nearer. The more he urged his horse, the further she was from him, though she rode no faster than before. When he saw it was pointless to follow her, he returned to Pwyll. 'Lord, the horse can do no more than you have seen.'

'She must be on an errand,' said Pwyll. 'Let us return to court.'

They spent that night in songs and feasting. The next day, when meat was ended, Pwyll said, 'Where are those that went yesterday and the day before to the top of the mound?

'We will go to the mound and sit there,' they said.

He turned to the page who tended his horse, 'Saddle my horse well, and hasten with him to the road, and also bring also my spurs.'

They went and sat on the mound; and after a short time, they saw the lady coming by the same road, in the same manner and pace. 'I see the lady coming; give me my horse,' said Pwyll. As soon as he was mounted, she passed him. He followed her, but he came no nearer. Urging his horse to his utmost speed, he still found it pointless.

Pwyll said, 'Oh maiden, wait for me.'

'I will wait gladly,' said she. 'It would have been better for your horse if you had asked before.'

So the maiden stopped, threw back the headdress covering her face, fixed her eyes on him, and began to talk with him. 'Lady,' asked he, 'where do you come from, and where are you going?'

'I journey on my own errand, and I am most glad to see you.'

'Will you not tell me your purpose?' said Pwyll.

'I will tell you,' she said. 'My chief quest was to seek you.'

'This is the most pleasing quest on which you could have come,' said Pwyll. 'Will you tell me who you are?'

'I am Rhiannon, the daughter of Hefeydd Hen. They sought to give me to a husband against my will. But I would have no husband because of my love for you. I have come to hear your answer.'

'If I could choose from all the ladies and damsels in the world, I would choose you,' said Pwyll.

'Indeed, then pledge to meet me before I am given to another.'

'Wherever you wish, I will meet with you there,' said Pwyll.

'I wish you to meet me this day in a year at the palace of Hefeydd. I will arrange a feast, so that it will be ready for your arrival.'

'Gladly,' said he.

'Lord,' she said, 'remain in health, and remember to keep your promise. Now I must leave.'

So they parted, and he returned to his household. Whatever questions they asked him about the damsel, he always turned conversation to other matters. When a year from that time was gone, he summoned a hundred knights to equip themselves and accompany him to the palace of Hefeydd Hen. He came to the palace, and there was great joy, with many people and great rejoicing at his coming. The whole Court was placed under his orders.

The hall was decked and they went to eat, Hefeydd Hen on one side of Pwyll, and Rhiannon on the other; then the rest according to their rank. They ate, feasted and talked. As the carousing after the meal began, there entered a tall auburn-haired youth, of royal bearing, clothed in satin. He entered the hall, saluting Pwyll and his companions. 'Greetings to you,' said Pwyll, full of good food, good wine and good cheer, 'come and sit.'

'No, I have come on an errand to crave a favour of you.'

'Whatever you ask of me, as far as I can, you shall have it.'

Rhiannon cried out in shock, 'Why did you give that answer?'

'He has given it before the presence of these nobles,' said the young man.

'What do you ask?' said Pwyll.

'The lady whom I love best is at your side. I come to ask for her.'

Pwyll was silent because of the answer which he had given.

'Be silent as long as you will,' said Rhiannon, taking Pwyll aside. 'A man never made worse use of his wits than you have done.'

'I did not know who he was,' said Pwyll.

'This is the man to whom they would give me against my will,' she said. 'He is Gwawl, the son of Clud, a man of great power and wealth. Because of the word you have given, you must promise me to him, lest shame befall you.'

'I do not understand your answer,' said Pwyll, 'I can never do as you say.'

'Make this promise to him,' she said, 'I will ensure that I shall never be his. I will give you a small bag; take care of it well. He will request a banquet and feast. I will arrange this feast, and engage to become his bride a year from tonight. In one year, you will be here. Bring this bag with you, and ensure your hundred knights are in the orchard. While he is feasting, come in by yourself wearing rags, holding the bag in your hand. Ask for nothing but a bagful of food. I will arrange that even if all the meat and drink that are in these seven Cantrefs were put into it, it would still not be full.

After a great deal has been put in, he will ask if the bag will ever be full. You must say that it never will, until a man of noble birth and great wealth presses the food in the bag with both feet. I will make him tread down the food in the bag. When he does so, pull the bag over his head, and then knot the thongs of the bag. Let there be also a good bugle about your neck, and as soon as you bind the bag, sound your horn to signal your knights. When they hear the horn, let them come down to the palace.'

'Lord,' said Gwawl impatiently, 'it is right that my request should be answered.'

'All that you have requested that is in my power to give, you shall have,' replied Pwyll.

'As for the feast and the banquet that are here,' Rhiannon said to him, 'I have bestowed them upon the men of Dyfed, and our household and warriors. I cannot permit them to be given to any other. A year from tonight a banquet shall be prepared for you in this palace, so that I may become your bride.'

So Gwawl departed, and Pwyll returned to Dyfed, and spent the year there until it was time for the feast at the palace of Hefeydd Hen. Then Gwawl, the son of Clud, arrived at the palace, and was received with rejoicing. Pwyll Pen Annwfn came to the orchard with his hundred knights, as Rhiannon had commanded, bringing the bag. Pwyll was clad in coarse rags, with large clumsy old shoes on his feet. When he heard carousing after the feast, he approached the hall, saluted Gwawl, the son of Clud, and his company. Gwawl greeted him. 'Lord,' said Pwyll, 'I ask to have this small bag here filled with food.'

'A reasonable request, this,' he said, 'and gladly you shall have it. Bring him food.' Many attendants rose to fill the bag. Yet for all that they put in, it was no fuller than at first. 'On my soul,' said Gwawl, 'will your bag ever be full?'

'It will not, unless someone with lands, domains and treasure treads down the food with both his feet, and says "Enough has been put in".'

Then Rhiannon said to Gwawl the son of Clud, 'Rise up quickly.' So he rose up, and put both feet into the bag.

Pwyll quickly turned the bag up over Gwawl's head, shut it quickly, and knotted the thongs. Then he blew his horn, and his knights came down to the palace. They seized all of Gwawl's men, casting them into the prison. Pwyll threw off his rags, his old shoes, and his tattered array.

As they arrived, every one of Pwyll's knights hit the bag, asking, 'What have we here?'

'A Badger!' they replied, each of them striking the bag with foot or staff.

Pwyll laughed, 'What game are you playing at here?'

'The game of Badger in the Bag,' came the knights' reply.

'Lord,' said the man in the bag, 'hear me. I do not merit being slain in a bag.'

Hefeydd Hen said, 'Listen to him. He does not deserve this.'

'This is my advice,' said Rhiannon. 'You should pay instead of him for the feast, give gifts for his minstrels and company, and make him swear he will never seek revenge for what has been done to him. That will be punishment enough.'

'I will do this,' said the man in the bag.

'I accept it gladly,' said Pwyll. Then Gwawl was let out of the bag and his kinsmen were liberated.

'I am greatly hurt, I have many bruises. I need ointment, I must depart. I will leave my nobles with you, to answer for me.' So Gwawl returned to his own lands.

The hall was set in order for Pwyll and his company and those of the palace. They sat at table as they had a year earlier, feasted, and spent the night in mirth and tranquillity. When the time came that they should sleep, Pwyll and Rhiannon went to their chamber, and passed the night in pleasure.

At the break of day, Rhiannon said, 'My Lord, arise and start to give your gifts to the minstrels. Refuse no one their fee.'

'Gladly,' said Pwyll, 'both today and every day while the feast lasts.' So Pwyll arose, called for silence, and commanded all suitors and minstrels to point out the gifts they wished and desired. This done, the feast proceeded, and he denied no one while it lasted.

With the feast ended, Pwyll said to Hefeydd, 'My Lord, with your permission I will set out for Dyfed tomorrow.'

So the next day, they set out for Dyfed, and journeyed to the palace of Narberth, where a feast was readied for them, attended by many of the chiefs and most noble ladies of the land. Rhiannon gave rich gifts to all: a bracelet, or ring, or precious stone.

Pwyll and Rhiannon ruled the land prosperously both that year and the next.

But in the third year, the nobles of the land began to be concerned to see a man whom they loved so much still without an heir. They came to him, meeting at Preseli in Dyfed. 'Lord,' they said, 'we know you are not as young as some of the men of this country. We fear that you may not have an heir from the wife you have taken. So take another wife who may give you heirs.'

'We have not long been joined together,' said Pwyll. 'Grant me a year from now. After that I will do as you wish.' So they granted it.

Before the end of a year a son was born to him in Narberth. On the night that he was born six women were brought into the chamber to watch over the mother and her boy. They watched for a good portion of the night, but before midnight every one of them fell asleep.

Towards break of day they awoke and looked for the boy, and beheld he was not there. 'Oh,' said a woman, 'the boy is lost!'

'Yes,' said another, 'and it will be small vengeance if we are burnt or put to death because of the child.'

Another asked, 'Is there any advice in the world for us?'

'There is here a stag-hound bitch with a litter of whelps,' one said, 'we will kill some of the cubs, rub the blood on the face and hands of Rhiannon, lay the bones by her, and claim she herself has devoured her son. She alone will not be able to gainsay us six.'

They agreed this between them. Towards morning Rhiannon awoke. 'Women, where is my son?'

'Lady,' they replied, 'do not ask us about your son, we have blows and bruises from struggling with you. We never saw a woman as violent as you. Did you not yourself devour your son?'

'For pity's sake,' said Rhiannon, 'do not charge me falsely. If you speak from fear, I will defend you.'

'Truly,' they said, 'we would not bring evil on ourselves for anyone in the world.'

'For pity's sake,' said Rhiannon, 'you must tell the truth.' But for all her pleading, she received the same answer from the women.

This event could not be concealed from Pwyll and his retinue. The story spread, and all the nobles heard it. They came to Pwyll, and pressed him to divorce his wife, for her great crime. But Pwyll answered them, that they had no cause save for her having no children. 'She has had a child, therefore I will not divorce her; if she has done wrong, let her do penance for it.'

So Rhiannon sent for the teachers and the wise men, and as she preferred doing penance to disputing with those women, she accepted a penance. The penance that was imposed was that she remain in that palace of Narberth for seven years; that every day she should sit by a mounting block at the gate, she should relate the story to all who passed and offer guests and strangers (if they would permit her) to carry them on her back into the palace.

Now at that time Teirnon Twrf Liant was Lord of Gwent Is Coed. To his house there belonged a mare – no mare or horse in the kingdom was more beautiful. On the eve of every first of May she foaled, though no one ever knew what became of the colt. One night Teirnon talked with his wife: 'Wife, it is very foolish of us that our mare foals every year, yet we have none of her colts.'

'What can be done?' said she.

'This is the eve of the first of May,' he said. 'I must learn what is removing the colts.' He had the mare brought into the house, armed himself, and began a night watch.

At the beginning of the night, the mare gave birth to a large and beautiful colt, and it was already standing up. Teirnon rose up and looked at the size of the colt, and as he did so heard a great tumult. Then he saw a claw come through the window into the house. It seized the colt by the mane. Teirnon drew his sword, and struck off the arm at the elbow, so the arm and the colt were indoors with him. Then he heard a tumult and wailing. He opened the door and rushed out in the direction of the noise. He could not see the cause because of the darkness of the night. He rushed after it and followed it, but then remembered that he had left the door open, and he returned. And at the door, behold, there was an infant boy in swaddling clothes, wrapped in a satin mantle. He took up the boy, and saw that he was very strong for his young age.

He took the boy to the chamber with his wife. 'Behold, here is a boy for you,' he said, 'since you never had one.'

'My lord,' said she, 'what adventure is this?' Teirnon told her how it all happened. She asked, 'What sort of garments are on the boy?'

'A satin mantle,' said Teirnon.

'Then he is of gentle lineage,' she replied. 'I will call my women unto me, and tell them that I have been pregnant.'

They did so, and then had the boy baptised. They named him Gwri Wallt Euryn, because his hair was as yellow as gold. Before the year was over, the boy could walk stoutly. He was larger than a boy of three years. The boy was nursed the second year, and then he was as large as a child of six years. Before the end of the fourth year, he was bribing the grooms to let him to take the horses to water.

'My lord,' said Teirnon's wife, 'where is the colt which you saved on the night that you found the boy?'

'I commanded the grooms to take care of him.'

'Would it not be well to have him broken in, and given to the boy, seeing that on the night that you found the boy, the colt was foaled and you saved him too?'

So the horse was given to the boy. The stable hands were commanded to care for the horse, breaking him in by the time that the boy could ride him.

As this was proceeding, they heard tidings of Rhiannon and her punishment. Teirnon Twrf Liant felt pity on hearing this story of Rhiannon and her punishment. Then Teirnon pondered within himself, and looked steadfastly at the boy. It seemed to him that he had never seen as great a likeness between father and son as between this boy and Pwyll Pen Annwfn.

He knew Pwyll's appearance well as he had formerly been one of his followers. He grieved for the wrong that he had done, keeping a boy whom he knew to be the son of another man. He told his wife that it was not right to keep the boy with them, whilst Rhiannon was punished so greatly, and when the boy was clearly the son of Pwyll Pen Annwfn.

Teirnon's wife agreed that they should send the boy to Pwyll. 'We shall gain three things, Lord,' said she, 'thanks and gifts for releasing Rhiannon from her punishment; thanks from Pwyll for nursing his son and restoring him to him; and thirdly, if the boy is of gentle nature, he will be our foster son, and will do all he can for us.' So it was settled.

So Teirnon, the boy mounted on his special horse, and two other members of his household, journeyed towards Narberth. As they approached the palace, they saw Rhiannon sitting beside the mounting block. She said 'Wait! I will carry every one of you into the palace, this is my penance for slaying my own son and devouring him.'

'Oh fair lady,' said Teirnon, 'I will not be carried upon your back.'

'Neither will I,' said the boy. So they continued to the palace, where there was great joy at their coming. A feast was being prepared because Pwyll had just returned from a tour of Dyfed. They went into the hall and washed, and Pwyll rejoiced to see Teirnon.

They sat Teirnon between Pwyll and Rhiannon, Teirnon's two companions on the other side of Pwyll, and the boy between them. After meat they began to carouse and converse. Teirnon related the adventure of the mare and the boy, how he and his wife had nursed and reared the child as their own. 'And here is thy son, lady,' said Teirnon, turning to Rhiannon. 'Whoever told that lie concerning you has done wrong. When I heard of your sorrow, I was troubled and grieved. I believe there is none of this company who will not recognise that the boy is the son of Pwyll.'

They all agreed, 'There is none who is not certain.'

'I declare,' said Rhiannon, 'that if this is true, there is indeed an end to my anxiety' – pryder was her word in Welsh.

'Lady,' said Pendaran Dyfed, 'you have well named your son Pryderi. His name becomes him well, Pryderi son of Pwyll Pen Annwfn.'

'But doesn't his original name suit him better?' asked Rhiannon.

'We named him Gwri Wallt Euryn,' said Teirnon.

'It is fine and appropriate,' said Pwyll, 'that the boy be named from the word his mother spoke when she received such joyful tidings of him.' It was agreed.

'Teirnon,' said Pwyll, 'I thank you for rearing the boy until now, and, it is fitting that he repays you for it.'

'My lord,' said Teirnon, 'it was my wife who nursed him, and no one in the world is as sad as she at parting with him. He should remember what I and my wife have done for him.'

'I declare that you shall both be foster parents to him,' said Pwyll.

Pryderi, the son of Pwyll Pen Annwfn, was brought up carefully as appropriate, and became the fairest youth, the most comely, and the best skilled in all good games, of any in the kingdom. And thus passed years and years, until Pwyll Pen Annwfn's life ended and he died.

Then Pryderi ruled the seven Cantrefs of Dyfed prosperously, beloved by his people.

So ends this branch of the Mabinogion.

We sat in silence for a few moments. Dusk had settled over the green mound at Narberth as the tale wound on. I stood up, and thanked him for such a story of great cruelties and great love. 'And now,' said the man, 'you also know that the 'Otherworld' is not in some faraway place, but right here under your feet.'

He paused, and I waited for him to continue. He took a deep breath, and said, 'Every day we come and go, busy with familiar faces and places.'

As he spoke he glanced over from the green mound to the familiar market cross in Narberth, busy with people coming and going in the early evening. Then he continued, 'But do we really know who they are? Why they are here? What they are doing?'

So many questions, but I still waited for the man to say more. However, now he remained silent. So I thanked him for all his stories thus far, and for helping me to a greater understanding of the Otherworld, especially with this latest tale. I realised now that this county of Pembrokeshire was of great importance in the relationship of the two worlds.

He looked at me with more respect, so I ventured further. Many of the objects which we are seeking have their place in stories. They have been included by many storytellers throughout time – in the oral tradition, in books and in drama and poetry. I gave some examples like *The Lord of The Rings*, the 'Narnia' stories and so on. He eyed me with a look that I was beginning to get used to. I quickly continued before he stopped me.

'So I understand that the objects are relevant to the stories. But I still don't see why we have to collect them, or why you have to take them back?'

'Because they are endangered,' he said.

I started to ask another question. But he changed the subject to the following day. There was no object to be exchanged or found, but he needed to consult. This was new. 'Who?' 'What?' 'How?' I asked, but as usual was silenced.

'Just wait and see,' was all he would venture.

'Where shall we meet?'

'Haverfordwest; the county town.'

I asked him where.

'The market.'

This could be tricky I thought. There was a weekly farmers' street market, and there was the rebuilt Riverside Market. I supposed both were probably too modern to be the right place for our needs. But as they were both by the river, we agreed to meet there. He now did something new: he asked for some money. I held out a handful of coins of various denominations from my purse. I wasn't sure what was wanted. He took the lot.

I ventured another guess at his name and asked him if it was Merbokey, since it was compiled from Mermaid, Box and Key, some of the items on his list. He shook his head, but with a grin rather than a frown. I wondered if I might be on to something.

As I made my way home I pondered more about the tokens he was seeking and about his description of them as 'endangered'. Again my thoughts broke into sleep and dreams that night.

# HAVERFORDWEST (HARFORD), HWLLFFORDD

The next day we met at Riverside Market. He had a big smile on his face and held up a small mirror. 'I bought it at the top of the hill in an antique shop. I found Market Street thinking that could be the right place, then turned the corner and lo and behold, an "Aladdin's Cave". The man who sold me this mirror let me have it half price. He knew a bit about its history, apparently once part of a larger mirror which has been re-framed. He bought the original at a sale, from a large house outside the town. It is just what I was looking for.'

I thought of stories which featured a mirror including Snow White and of course *Through the Looking Glass*. But then I remembered, 'I thought you said that there was no token here?'

'I need to place this somewhere and then gain some knowledge.'

I found it difficult to contain my questions, but my companion was clearly the guardian of some knowledge that he had to keep to himself and I had to respect that. It didn't stop them forming in my mind though. I also realised that I could build my own stories around some of the valuable insights I was gaining on the journey. In the old tradition of the storyteller, if you don't know, you just make it up.

He told me some things that I didn't know about Hwllffordd (Haverfordwest – often called Harford by locals).

## HAVERFORDWEST CASTLE

A famous robber was held in chains in one of the towers at the Castle of Haverfordwest. Three children were allowed to visit the robber frequently in his tower: the son and grandson of the lord of the castle, and the son of the Earl of Clare. They asked him to give them arrows, which he made for them. The children learnt much from the robber, who was clever and amusing. One day the three boys asked the gaoler to bring the robber from his tower into an anteroom. The gaoler left the robber with the children for just a few moments. Taking advantage of the gaoler's absence, the robber took the children back to the tower and locked them in with him.

The alarm was raised; everyone in the castle was alerted. The boys were yelling to be rescued. The robber raised an axe and threatened the lives of the children. The lord of the castle had to promise a pardon for his crime and allow him free passage, before the children were returned unharmed to him.

I told my friend a recent story about two young women in Haverfordwest.

## THE SILENT TWINS

June and Jennifer were identical twins. Shortly after their birth in Barbados, their family moved to Haverfordwest. As they grew up it became clear that the girls, who were inseparable, had speech problems. This is quite common with twins who become used to understanding each other and sometimes develop their own language. It was almost impossible for anyone outside the family to understand them.

When the time came for them to go to school, life became very difficult for the twins. They were ostracised by other children who found them strange and difficult to communicate with.

The twins were sent home early each day to help them avoid bullying from other children outside the school gates. Their language became even more unintelligible to outsiders; indeed they stopped speaking to anyone else.

A succession of therapists and specialists tried to get them to communicate with others, but without success. At fourteen it was decided that they should go to separate boarding schools in an attempt to break their isolation. This separation made them both distraught. They felt that they had each lost part of themselves. They could not bear to be parted and had no one to speak to.

They were reunited and spent two years in their bedroom, playing with dolls and creating stories. Many of the stories were recorded on a tape recorder for their little sister.

Someone in the family bought them both diaries, which sparked an interest in writing. They enrolled in a mail-order course in creative writing, and then each wrote several novels. They both wrote in a unique personal style.

They self-published using a vanity press and made many attempts to sell short stories to magazines, but were unsuccessful. In an effort to gain recognition and fame and thereby publicity for their books, the girls committed a number of petty crimes. This didn't seem to have the effect that they required, so they moved on to more serious crime and were found guilty of arson. Both were committed to Broadmoor, a high security mental health hospital.

The two women remained there for fourteen years. Their diary-keeping continued. They both joined the hospital choir, but no more stories came from their pens.

The twins had long agreed that if one of them died, the surviving twin would start to speak to others. They began to think that it was necessary for one of them to die. It seems that Jennifer agreed to become the sacrifice, and shortly after they were released from Broadmoor, she died of sudden inflammation of the heart. There was no evidence of drugs or poison in her system. To this day, Jennifer's death remains a mystery.

Only then, after Jennifer's death, was June able to speak with other people, giving interviews to newspapers and magazines. She became much more communicative and moved away from Haverfordwest.

My companion had a stiff impenetrable look on his face, and made no comment about this story. I thought perhaps he didn't want to hear such a tale from our own times. I thought it strange and sad, but perhaps it was not to his taste. But once again my companion surprised me. 'I thought that was marvellous,' he said.

'You do?'

'Yes, you understand that Pembrokeshire, this very special place, is always really two places. This world and the Otherworld. The land that becomes sea and princes that become pigs. Strong wenches and green mermaids. Storytellers talking and shepherds lost for speech. Good saints and wicked criminals.'

I was silent now. My friend had never been so moved. He continued, 'Now I will tell you a tale of someone else from Haverfordwest who sailed the seas, and walked the line between doing good and being bad, just like your twins.'

## PIRATE JOHN CALLICE

John Callice sailed the seas from Pembrokeshire to the Barbary Coast, one of the most flamboyant and wealthy pirates of his time.

When he was a young man he left his home in Haverfordwest and journeyed to London to seek his fortune. He worked in a shop, but there was no fortune to be made in this work. Long days and low wages barely gave him a living. So, he decided to join the Royal Navy.

He soon found his sea legs and loved his life as a sailor. He worked his way through the ranks with astonishing speed and within three years achieved the command of a Royal Navy ship.

Shortly after his appointment as commander, he seized an Italian merchant vessel. He brought the cargo to Pembrokreshire and sold it here. Callice normally disposed of his booty in Wales, where local landowners and royal officials and even the Vice-Admiral were well known to him. His new career as a pirate had begun. Over the next four years he plundered countless merchant ships.

In 1577 Callice was caught and charged with six counts of piracy. He was imprisoned in London and after his trial was sentenced to hang, but his influential friends intervened and James VI of Scotland persuaded Queen Elizabeth I to pardon him. After his release he left Britain and it was reported that he had become a reformed character.

In 1582 he was commissioned to assist in arresting pirates at sea. Using reformed pirates to catch others in piracy was common practice. But Callice did not honour this agreement, instead pirating two Scottish merchant vessels, and selling their cargo at Portsmouth. He kept one of the captured ships for his own and christened it 'The Golden Chalice'; this is probably a pun on his name.

Hounded by the authorities he soon abandoned his ship and in 1584 joined Captain Fenner, who had been granted a licence to take Spanish and Portuguese ships as prizes of war. But Callice couldn't resist taking control of a captured warship, in which he sailed away to spend his last years in piracy off the Barbary Coast. Eventually he was killed in battle and buried at sea.

'Was Harford a hotbed of pirates?' I asked. 'There seem to be many stories about piracy.'

'I can tell you many, but here is just one more for now,' he said.


## CONTRABAND

In the sixteenth century Haverfordwest became the centre for illegal trading in all manner of goods. Participants in the trade included admirals, priests, municipal officers, saddlers, victuallers and even customs men themselves.

The town became notorious. The government in England issued a commission to Sir John Perrot, Vice-Admiral for west Wales, to suppress the pirates and the illegal trading. It had little effect.

When ships came into harbour, everyone, including the Mayors of Haverfordwest, Pembroke and Tenby, traded openly with the pirates. Even Sir John's own servant turned pirate and commanded a ship called *The Elephant*, which often sailed into port with wines, salt, grain and dried fish. It was known that many a tun of Gascon wine found its way into the cellars of Sir John Perrot.

## MARTIN DAVY'S STONE (HANGSTONE DAVY)

But not all wrongdoers got away with their crimes. About halfway between Haverfordwest and Little Haven, on the southern side of the road where it crosses a common, is a small upright stone, not much larger than a milestone. You can miss it unless you know what to look for.

By tradition it is known as Martin Davy's Stone. A man of this name stole a sheep one night, and was carrying it home from Haverfordwest on his shoulders with its four feet tied together. Tiring, he sat down at this stone to rest, putting his back against it. Gradually he fell asleep, slipping down the stone. The animal was then lying on top of him. The sheep, becoming uncomfortable, gave a convulsive movement; its legs slipped down in front of the man's throat, and its body slipped down behind the stone.

The thief suddenly woke up. He was trapped; he could not raise the sheep's body up high enough to escape. He was found the next day throttled to death in this position.

After this rather gruesome piece, to change the subject I asked my companion if his name was associated with the objects we were seeking, or perhaps was it included in one of the stories so far. 'I can't help, it is against the rules.'

'What rules?' I began. But he interrupted me and said that we must meet the following day at Roch, by the castle. I searched in my rucksack for a map to be sure of the location. When I brought it out, he had gone. I still hadn't seen him arrive or leave at any of our meeting places. I had no idea how he travelled, but I did have plenty of food for thought about our quest.

# ROCH

When I arrived at the castle, my companion was waiting with an impatient air about him. He asked me to carry the basket. We looked at the Castle which had been beautifully restored.

He told me its legend.

## THE LEGEND OF ROCH CASTLE

You already know that Pembrokeshire is always two places. The Landsker is yet another way that this magical place shows two faces to the world. In the south, the face speaks English, in the north, beyond the Landsker, it speaks Welsh. The Landsker – you can't see it but you can hear it – crosses Pembrokeshire from the south-east, near Amroth, to the north-west here at Roch. And right here stands Roch Castle.

In the thirteenth century, the feudal Lord Adam de la Roche had a premonition that a year from the foretelling, he would die from an adder's sting. So he built the castle and lived in apartments at the very top of the tower, never venturing out to avoid the possibility of encountering a snake or indeed any other sort of animal. The year passed, and people started to celebrate his survival. Winter came and a bitter wind blew. A servant brought firewood into the the apartments. He made up the fire and put a sturdy log pile beside it. The fire was lit and his lordship sat before the fire to warm himself. He fell asleep. An adder crept from the log pile and stung him. In the morning he was found in the chair beside the fire, dead.

'I heard that you can still buy the Lordship of the Manor of Roch,' I said.

My friend said, 'it just shows the power of tales and legends. I'm not interested as I am already a lord.'

I looked at him curiously, and he must have realised he had spoken too much. Changing the subject he said, 'Tomorrow we must meet at Druidstone, and there we must seek a whistle, as used by hunters and beaters to flush out game.'

He described the whistle. I told him that I had seen something which fitted that description in the window of a shop in Fishguard. The next day I bought it and took it with me to St Bride's Bay.

# DRUIDSTONE, LLECH Y DERWYDD

'Perfect,' he said, when we met. It was the nearest he had got to real praise in this whole journey. He blew on it and it sounded shrill. As we sat near a curious building covered in grass and facing straight out to the Atlantic Ocean, a startled bird flew over and dropped its tail feather. My friend ran to the spot as it drifted down, and picked it up.

'Perfect,' he said again and put the feather into the basket and the whistle in his pocket. He then asked me to carry the basket as it was getting too heavy for him.

He spoke of a young man who had come from here.

## THE TRAGEDY OF LLECH Y DERWYDD

There was a boy in Llech y Derwydd, the only child of his parents and sole heir to the farm. For them, he was the very sun and moon, the light of their eyes. He and the head servant, an orphan, were best friends, like two brothers, or rather twins. They were close in age and even looked alike, but that may have been because the boy's mother dressed them alike.

They spent all their time together and it happened that they both fell in love at the same time with two young women, both handsome and of good reputation. The boy's parents were very happy and agreed to arrange a double wedding. The merrymaking which followed the wedding ceremony was great. The son brought his new wife back to the farm and the servant brought his new wife to a small cottage on the farm that was made available to him.

Some months after the wedding the son and his friend went out hunting. They split up so that the servant could flush out some game to make good sport. The servant used a whistle to scare out several birds and a fox. But he heard no shot, so he emerged from a brushwood pile to where he had left his master, horrified to find that he was gone. The servant whistled and called him, but there was no answer. He searched and searched but his friend and master was nowhere to be seen. The sun was setting over St Bride's Bay when he finally abandoned the search and returned to the farm. He hoped that the young man would have already returned. But no one had heard or seen him. Nor did he return that night. The next day the father and servant went to the place where the young man had last been seen. They searched and searched, thinking that perhaps he had sustained a fall and had been injured. The circle of their search got wider and wider but he was not to be found.

They returned to the farm, again hoping that he had returned whilst they had been searching, but he was not there. The family was in great distress. His wife and mother and the servant's wife were crying bitterly and it seemed that they could not stop. The father and servant went around the neighbourhood to see if anyone had heard or seen him. No one had.

The following day at daybreak, the father and the servant returned again to the spot, wanting to continue the search rather than sit at home and grieve. They probably also felt that the sound of the women's weeping was not helpful. Once again they inspected the last spot where the son had been seen. To their great surprise they saw a fairy ring. They looked at each other, and the father shook his head in sorrow. Now the servant remembered that he had heard faint music as he parted from his friend. He had not thought twice about it at the time, but now it seemed important. He told the father, and they agreed that the farmer's son and heir must have entered the fairy ring and been transported to the Otherworld.

Days, weeks and months went by, with no news. Then through the sadness came joy; a son was born to the young man's wife in his absence. He grew up the very image of his father. Every time his mother looked at him she felt joy and also sadness. She missed her husband, who might never see his little boy. But no one heard from him. The grandparents doted on the child; it was some compensation for the loss of their son.

Many years passed, and the grandson grew up. The pretty young woman who was his childhood sweetheart was now his wife. His mother was concerned as her new daughter-in-law's family had a reputation for cruelty. Indeed it was a wonder that their daughter was so kind and loving.

The young man and his wife moved to Llech y Derwydd, and she helped to look after his mother and ageing grandparents. Eventually the old man died. Within weeks he was joined by his wife who could not bear to be without him.

There was great sadness in the home. But there was a farm to run and eventually children to look after; plenty to keep them all occupied. Eventually the boy's grieving mother also died, and his wife came into her own and enjoyed being mistress of the house. Something of her real nature now showed itself, as she became less kind, patient and loving, and harsher in her nature.

One windy afternoon in autumn, a man was seen walking towards the house. He was very thin, had a long beard and hair as white as snow. The family were shocked as he opened the door without a 'By your leave'. The mistress was angry. The children hid.

Then the children came out of hiding one by one and looked at the old man. He sat in their grandpa's chair by the fire and lifted the children up one by one to have a good look at them. He asked after his parents and his wife. Everyone was mystified. The wife thought he must be drunk and asked what his business was. He looked at the small children who had, in the way of children, accepted the fact that he sat in grandpa's chair by the fire and were already playing a game on the floor by his feet. The man looked mystified. He looked at the wife and explained that he had been out hunting only yesterday, been out for just one night, and now he had returned. Where were his parents? Where was his wife? He started to get angry.

She looked in disbelief at the old man. She and her husband well knew the story of his father who had gone out hunting, and who had been spirited away by the little people. They had been sceptical and thought that the parents had believed the story told by locals because they could not bear to think that he had been killed, which is what the young couple had always assumed.

Then the old man, agitated, got up, looked around the room, asked after things which had been moved, and asked angrily who these people were in his house. The young wife now became angry and afraid for her children. She shouted at the old man, obviously an impostor, telling him to leave. Alarmed, he left the house, and walked to the servant's cottage. Here he found an old man by the fire, and asked who he was. Where was his friend, his servant?

The man by the fire told once again the story of his lost master the son of Llech y Derwydd, and as he recalled the tale, the realisation dawned on him that he was speaking to the very man. His lost master had returned.

Now they remembered together the events of their youth and they knew each other. The servant broke the news to his friend and master that he had been gone for fifty years, that the farm was now owned and managed by his son and his wife, who now lived there with their children.

The returned son told of his time with the fairies, which he knew as just the day before. He stood up in bewilderment, and caught sight of himself in the mirror. The truth was reflected back to him.

His friend persuaded him to eat with him and his wife and to spend the night with him in his small cottage. He promised that the next day they would go together to Llech y Derwydd to tell the story of what had happened.

They sat at the table to eat a good meal. Afterwards the returned son of Llech y Derwydd stood up, stretched, thanked his host and the wife who had cooked for them. It was the best meal he had had since … and as he was trying to find words for the passage of time, he dropped down dead.

The faithful servant insisted that his returned master be buried with his parents and wife.

Two-and-a-half weeks after the funeral, when the moon rose full over St Bride's Bay, the mistress of the family farm was visited by a group of small people. They told her that her bad manners and poor treatment of the returned son had brought a curse upon the place. It would not be lifted until the farm had changed hands nine times.

This seemed a rather harsh punishment I thought, wondering if I would have behaved much better than the young wife. But the question that I was forming was quickly cut short.

'Tomorrow we must be careful,' I was instructed. Our meeting place was Broadhaven. When I turned to ask why and how, he had gone. I wasn't sure what was the required object, but perhaps he had that in hand.

# BROADHAVEN

Broadhaven was once a picturesque spot on the coast. I was anticipating salty sea tales. But as ever my expectations were upturned. Here is the story I was told.

## THE BROADHAVEN TRIANGLE

It began in February 1977. A group of children were playing football outside the primary school. Suddenly they saw a yellow cigar-shaped object fly through the air and land in the field behind the school. They ran indoors and told the head teacher. He was sceptical, especially as playtime was over, and it was time for the children to come in and get on with their work. When the children persisted, he relented and asked them to sketch what they had seen. He was astonished at how similar all the drawings were.

A few days later, the same craft was seen by three teachers at the school. News of these extraordinary sightings reached the ears of a local ufologist and journalist, who brought it to the attention of the national media. Subsequently, UFO spotters descended on Broadhaven with cameras, telescopes and notepads.

In March a young man saw a glowing orange disc in the sky over Broadhaven. At the same time a black dog ran past him. Then he saw a large dome-shaped object in a nearby field. A tall man with high cheekbones and wearing a one-piece suit walked towards him. He was afraid and hit out at him, but his fist hit nothing. Later when he got home, the family dog growled and barked at him as if he was a stranger.

In Milford Haven at around this time a seventeen-year-old girl reported seeing a 3ft-high creature sitting on her window sill looking in at her.

In April the owner of the Haven Fort Hotel in nearby Little Haven said that she was woken up in the early hours of the morning by strange sounds and lights outside. She got out of bed and looked out of the window to see a huge saucer-like shape in the field next to the hotel. Nearby she saw two faceless creatures with pointed heads; she also felt an intense heat. She also saw flames of all colours coming from the craft.

She cried out to the creatures, but there was no response. She called other people in the hotel to come and look, but when they reached the spot, the craft and the creatures had disappeared.

The next day the hotel owner went to look at the area where she had seen the craft and found flattened grass and scorch marks. She contacted her MP, who phoned the nearby RAF camp. The squadron leader came to see her, told her there was nothing at the camp which could account for the strange craft and suggested that she had probably seen workers from one of the local oil refineries, wearing protective suits. He asked her not to tell anyone about the sighting, as it could cause alarm amongst the public.

At Ripperstone Farm, during the course of a year, the family reported a series of unexplained phenomena. The wife was chased by a glowing object whilst driving home and cattle were mysteriously moved from one field to another. Also, electrical items in the house switched themselves on and off without explanation.

The mother and children returned to the house after going to a children's party to find their father in a nervous state having seen a strange silver car approach the house. A black-suited occupant approached the house, but he refused to go to the door since he thought that there was something strange about the occupants of the car. The next-door neighbour saw them too. She was putting out rubbish and saw one of the men. She described him as having strange, waxy skin, a high forehead, slicked back black hair, and cold, unblinking eyes. She went back indoors and the phone rang. It was a friend phoning to say she had just seen a strange looking silver car with two dark-suited men sitting inside. As the car left it made no noise on the gravel.

As my companion stopped speaking, schoolchildren came out into the playground. The noise made by such a small group was quite shrill. My companion went into the schoolyard and approached a boy with red hair. I started to worry; my friend was about the same size as the children and I lost sight of him with all the running, skipping and singing games. The next thing I knew he was at my side.

The token that my friend showed me was surprising. It was a toy car of silver-coloured metal. 'Where did you get that?' I asked.

'I swapped the whistle for it,' he smiled. Each day and each place presented new riddles and twists and turns.

I volunteered my latest guess about his name: 'Rhys Morgan'. He asked me how I arrived at that. I explained that I had taken the objects so far and drawn some of the letters out then rearranged them into this name. I looked hopeful; he hadn't shaken his head or laughed. Eventually he looked at me and said it was clever, but not right.

'But by coincidence tomorrow we are to meet at the harbour in Milford Haven, by a boat named the *Rhys Morgan*.'

'What must I bring?'

'A raincoat.'

# MILFORD HAVEN, ABERDAUGLEDDAU

The following day was blowing a westerly gale, with rain lashing on the quayside. I was glad of the raincoat. The object, my friend now revealed, was a length of rope from an old rig. He said that he had seen the very piece of rope he sought; it had been found by an artist and turned into a frame for an artwork. It was in a gallery down by the docks. 'But you will need to bargain for it,' he said. 'We will meet outside later, and you can go in. I may get trapped there.'

I had never seen fear in his face before, I asked him to explain but he changed the subject, and while we sheltered from the rain in the lee of the *Rhys Morgan*, tied up on the quayside, he told me a salty tale.

## CABIN BOY

Once there was a sailor called Tom, little more than a lad. He had left home at thirteen to make way for his brothers and sisters, and to earn some money for his poor widowed mother. He had managed to get a job as a cabin boy aboard a ship. The captain was a strict man, but mostly fair. By the time he was fourteen, the boy had visited many places, sailed many seas, learned how to dodge the anger of his fellow sailors and how to be useful on board ship. He rarely suffered the sickness that laid low many a rough, tough hairy seaman, which enabled him to curry favour with the first mate.

He liked nothing better than to listen to the yarns of the older men as they sat below deck in the evening, lighting their pipes and drinking rum. It seemed that the Pembrokeshire coast had always been a busy seafaring place, with many inlets and islands, and a retired sea dog in every cove. A number of older men told stories of piracy and of mermaids, of the green meadows of enchantment lying in St George's Channel to the west of Pembrokeshire, only visible to the eyes of mortals for a brief moment before vanishing. Some spoke of sailors who actually landed on the fairy islands, without realising where they were until they returned to their boats and watched with horror to see the recently visited island evaporate into thin air.

They said that the fairies living on these islands regularly came on shore for the markets at Milford Haven. They made their purchases without speaking, laid down their money and departed, always leaving the exact sum required, which they somehow knew.

Mostly the fairies were invisible, but just occasionally they were seen. One particular butcher in Milford Haven was especially favoured by fairy customers, who always knew the price of his sausages. Milford Haven folk were able to see the green fairy islands distinctly, just a short distance from land, and even to make out their population of fairies. They explained that they came to and fro between the islands and Milford through a tunnel under the seabed.

The time had come to collect the old rope. We walked over to the gallery which had once been a sailmaker's loft. There was a window at ground-floor level with some items displayed there but the main exhibits were upstairs. He explained where I could find the rope frame and waited outside. I was a bit worried about him and looked out of the window upstairs. He had crossed back over the road, and was now standing at the edge of the quay watching ships manoeuvring through the dock.

The gallery was run by a group of local artists, and had many beautiful items on show, but I couldn't see anything like the frame which my companion had described.

I asked the gallery manager. He said that it had been sold the day before. My heart sank. I asked if it was possible to find out who had bought the item and said it was important that I knew. The gallery manager looked at me suspiciously and told me that there were other items by the same artist if I was interested. I explained that it was the rope frame that interested me. 'In that case, you may be in luck,' he said. He picked up the phone and dialled a number then waited.

I was very anxious. I couldn't explain the urgency. If I had explained, he might have made another phone call and I might be carted off for treatment. What if there was no answer?

What if he had sold all the rope? There were lots more what-ifs in my mind when it became clear that someone had answered the phone.

Dai, the gallery manager, replaced the phone. He asked me to wait because the artist was coming in straight away. Worried that it may take too long, I asked, 'Will it be a long wait?' He assured me that this particular artist lived on a boat down in the marina, only a bike ride away. I went outside to inform my companion. He said he could see the artist approaching. Yet again it seemed that I didn't have to explain.

The artist greeted my companion as an old friend. He pulled out of his pocket a length of rope and gave it to him. My friend thanked the artist and looked at me with a look that said 'hurry'. I called my thanks upstairs to the gallery manager, and we left without another word. I looked back to see the artist waving goodbye to us, with the gallery manager at his side. It was only then that I noticed that the artist was a man of small stature. I looked at my companion, who was smiling.

I felt sure that I understood very little of what was going on.

By now the rain had eased and a patch of blue sky was appearing over the Haven. We found a bench at the end of the Rath, from where the neighbouring town of Neyland was clearly visible. I took the rope and laid it over the wet seat for us to sit down. Then I told my friend some anecdotes about Neyland.

# NEYLAND

Neyland is a very special place; people who come to live here soon gain a great affinity with the history and the place. The town is built very much on the industry of fish. Not just fishing boats but an ice factory for packaging for the transportation of fish, and a railway line with trains for passengers, freight and post. I was told by one of the older residents that as children they were often sent running down to the station with an urgent letter or parcel to catch the post.

Neyland once boasted its own cinema: a corrugated iron building. Local children used to delight in running along it with a stick to create a terrible noise whilst the film was being screened, disturbing the audience. They ran away quickly before they were caught.

My friend told me that he used to attend this cinema. Cowboy films were always popular. The milkman used to ride into town on his carthorse and tether it outside when he watched the latest Western.

My companion was amazing. I asked him how old he was. He wouldn't say. I had another guess at his name. Was it Ryxne? It was made up from the third letter in each of the objects in our quest so far. He laughed. It was a laugh of pleasure rather than scorn, so I thought that maybe I was thinking correctly. It was a bit like doing a cryptic crossword and I was never very good at those, and he was clearly not going to give me a hint.

Sore from sitting on the hard rope, I stood up, and asked where next.

'Redberth.'

I had never heard of it. 'Where is it and what do we need to find?'

'Nothing, ' he replied, 'I must place something there.'

After some persuasion, my companion agreed to reveal it was on the road from Kilgetty to Pembroke. Eventually I found the place on the map. On my way home I reflected again on the quest. The quantity of tokens seemed more than I had ever encountered in any one story before. So often stories work by the rule of three, which can mean three attempts to reach a destination or conclusion, or three characters who provide three different ways. Sometimes there are the magic sevens: seven champions; seven children; seven dwarfs and so on. I have a theory that these stepping stones of seven represent the phases of maturity, the leaps that humans take at the age of seven, fourteen, twenty-one and so on through life. Each of the objects so far appeared in the stories that I regularly told, so they seemed like familiar friends. I mentally listed everything in the basket: silver hairs; key; box; ring; bread; candlestick; feather; toy car; and rope. Clearly it was more than seven.

I thought more about what the tokens might signify or represent. I had reached home before I had assembled my thoughts. The artefacts all represented elements of life and of stories. There used to be a radio programme when I was a child called *Animal, Vegetable or Mineral*, and it seemed then that everything could be pigeonholed in this way. Now I wondered. My thoughts took me no further and certainly no closer to his name or the essence of the quest. But the stories were a real bonus. Such a variety of tales was proving to be good material for my book and the tokens we found all made fine cues for tales.

# REDBERTH

The next day at midday, he was standing at the roadside in this tiny hamlet looking at an old dilapidated barn which had an estate agent's board attached to it. Judging by my companion's interest, it seemed to be a significant place, though judging by the rubble piled up outside, it was suffering from neglect.

I asked him how he felt about it being bought and developed. 'I am happy that it will be preserved,' he said. He told me a story.

Once there was a family, hardworking and poor but proud. They were called Sam and Mai Thomas, and their children were Llew who was twelve, Sarah aged ten, and Tilly, who was six years old. They lived in a tiny cottage, one room up and two rooms down.

They all worked hard. Sam was a cooper and Mai baked bread and brewed ale. All the children helped their parents. Their neighbours were all hardworking. There was a shoemaker, a tailor, a blacksmith, a mason and a shipwright. Others worked in local quarries. At the end of a hard, thirsty day in the quarry they would stop by for a pint of ale brewed by Mai. On many occasions when sales of Sam's barrels were slow, Mai's brewing and baking kept them fed. Sometimes barter would take place between members of the community. A barrel of beer would pay for a new pair of boots or a shirt. They also had more wealthy customers. The well-heeled Barlow family of Lawrenny ordered new hunting boots, several barrels, new stirrups or livery for their footmen. At other times, Llewhellin Priday, who was an owner-occupier with four acres, had farm implements repaired or his horse shod.

The Ashleys of the Lodge were good customers in the community before they moved to Tenby, particularly when old Mrs Ashley died and they ordered a headstone for the grave from the mason. Everyone shared in these moments of good fortune, but there were times when these customers were slow in paying their bills. This had a devastating effect on the small village of Redberth, but neighbours rallied round and looked after each other. Frequently the smith, the mason or the shoemaker would have a pint 'on tick' if they were waiting for a bill to be paid and needed to slake their thirst on a hot sunny day. All in all, everything worked out fairly; no one went hungry, although some went without boots or a Sunday suit.

One winter, when the days were short and the weather cold, Sam was on his way to Haverfordwest market with some barrels on his cart. He was hoping that the sale of these barrels would give him enough cash to buy oak to make new barrels and to pay his bill at the smiths. His son Llew accompanied him; Llew was learning the craft of the cooper from his father.

Suddenly disaster struck. The carthorse caught its foot in a rut which had been made by a heavy carriage passing by in the autumn.

When the cold weather came, frost caused the furrow and the ridge to become frozen. The wheel of the cart got caught in the furrow and the horse stumbled, turning the cart over on the hard ground and trapping Sam underneath. Llew ran to fetch help. Neighbours rallied round and set the cart right but the barrels were badly damaged and the cart needed repair. Luckily the horse, a sturdy Welsh cob, was frightened but sound. But lying lifeless on the ground, Sam was dead.

It was the worst thing that Llew had ever had to do, before or since. He had to return home to tell his mother that her husband, his father, was dead! The poor woman was distraught. He was a good husband and father; hardworking, ever-loving – she missed him every day for the rest of her life.

A funeral was arranged, and the mason made a suitable memorial stone, saying that Mai could pay him later, and the community celebrated the life of Sam Thomas the cooper.

Without Sam's income the family struggled to make ends meet. Mai baked and brewed; she grew what she could in their small garden, but now the family often went to bed hungry. The rent didn't get paid and eventually the landlord had no choice but to give notice to quit. He was a kindly man and didn't like to turn the family out on the street, but he had to make ends meet too and relied on the rent from his cottages to earn his living.

The shoemaker and the mason had both had a run of good luck. Along with the blacksmith and the shipwright, they decided to pay the rent owing on the cottage. They set it up as an alehouse so that Mai could brew her delicious beer and sell it from the cottage. Nearly everyone in the small community was delighted, and the tradespeople who had provided the money to set up the alehouse were very satisfied with their investment. The landlord was relieved to get his back rent and to see Mai and her family making a reasonable living. He even had the occasional free pint.

There was one person, however, who was not best pleased. Ann Pitney Thomas had tenanted the Lodge after the Ashleys moved to Tenby. She came to Redberth following the death of her father, the Rev. Seth Jones Thomas. Born at Begelly Rectory, she was the youngest daughter of the rector. Her background inclined her to good works, often distributing bibles and occasionally a loaf of bread. Her mother had a connection in early life with John Wesley and she felt that she was continuing a tradition. She was involved in the rebuilding of the church, and was a key figure in the foundation and management of the school. Something of a puritan, it was to her satisfaction that there was no public house in Redberth.

However the story about the cooper's wife came to her ears and she was determined to put a stop to it. She called by, bringing a bible, and spoke to Mai, trying to persuade her that it was a sin to sell alcohol. But Mai explained that this was the means by which she kept her family fed. Her brew was made from the best ingredients. Working people enjoyed a pint at the end of a hard day. She was not to be persuaded.

Anne Pitney Thomas tried to put off the customers without success. After many months of trying, she realised she was beaten, and abandoned her attempt to make Redberth a teetotal village.

However if she visited today she would be gratified to learn that there is no pub or alehouse, or even an off-licence in Redberth.

My companion picked his way through the rubble and the mountain of old paint tins and went into the old barn. He was inside for a few moments, while I waited outside. Some of the inhabitants eyed me oddly and came past several times to check on me. When I looked in the basket I saw that the mirror was missing.

Our next place was Orielton. I was getting to know this county very well. The items to be found locally were ramsons (wild garlic), sage, rosemary and thyme.

# ORIELTON

We met just outside the school. My companion was amused that the school was decorated in 'found' materials and objects and that the emblem on the children's school clothing was a seagull. 'You can find that story out for yourself,' he told me. He showed me that he had already picked the herbs. I was once more handed the basket, which made me feel nervous. He was no respecter of property, and I was colluding in whatever theft he had made to gain this part of his collection. He did, however tell me another tale from here.

## UNCLEAN SPIRITS

Once, long ago, in Orielton, there was a family called Wiriet — Stephen Wiriet, his wife Emma, and their children John and Sarah. Stephen had a joinery workshop, employing three carpenters and an apprentice. They mostly made window frames and coffins. It was a successful business, and they had been able to move from their small cottage to a larger house and employ a couple of maids to help with the cleaning and laundry.

One evening, after a fine meal which they shared with Stephen's brother Sam and his wife Jane, the family and their guests retired for the night, but were woken by noises downstairs. Thinking that thieves had entered the house, Stephen and his wife and their two guests came downstairs to see a man standing in the hallway of their home.

When Stephen challenged the man asking him to leave, the man shouted and swore at him and issued a stream of accusations. He questioned how he was now a wealthy man but once he had been poor, implying that he had obtained his wealth dishonestly. He claimed that one of the maids had been dallying with the butcher's boy. He alleged that his wife entertained the milkman in the kitchen every day. He claimed that when Stephen was a boy he had bitten his sister on the arm; and more recently that one of their children had stolen apples from the neighbour's orchard; and that stolen property was in the cupboard under the stairs.

Nothing they could say would stop the accusations and swearing. Stephen and his brother tried to eject the man from the house, but found that the presence was not human. It had no bodily substance.

Three nights running the same events occurred. Sometimes the spirit asked why Stephen had once been wealthy and was now poor, quite the opposite of what was alleged on the previous evening. The intruder questioned the honesty of every member of the household and taunted them with stories of private matters and embarrassing incidents which had occurred to each member of the family since birth, and which they were not willing to be heard by others.

After several days of this abuse, it stopped as suddenly as it started. Shortly afterwards they heard from a neighbour, one William Nott. He complained that unclean spirits had entered his house, had thrown dirt at the occupants and followed this up by cutting holes in linen and wool garments. New locks and bolts were fitted to all the doors but these were no barriers to the spirits.

A priest was called to purify both houses with holy water, but even as the priest was exorcising the homes, the spirit arrived to abuse him in like fashion. Both families moved away, and their houses fell into disrepair.

Generations later, another house was built on that land. The woman living there was said to be possessed by an evil spirit, which used her voice to taunt members of the household, to argue with visitors, and to reveal secrets that people would rather have remained hidden. Holy men and wise people were called to rid this woman of the evil spirit. They placed holy relics and potions in her mouth.

The devil fled to the lower part of her throat. When the holy relics and potions were removed, the spirit descended to her belly. As he moved through her body it was seen to inflate and convulse with the movement.

When the relics were placed in the lower parts, the devil directly returned to the upper part. It wasn't until a wise woman cleared the room, gave some herbs to the woman and sat with her whilst she slept that the poor creature was rid of the evil possessor of her body.

Our next visit was to Maenclochog. The object we needed to find was a chess piece. I told him that I had a chess set that my father had found when I was a child. The pieces were very old, and as children we were just as fascinated by the old leather shirt-collar box in which they were kept. I still keep them in that same box. 'Bring them,' he said. 'I need to see them.'

I had another go at his name, 'Simon Segmex'. I was quite pleased with this, I thought that it had a musical quality to it. When he asked how I had arrived at the name I said that I had made a list of collected objects, then taken the first letter of the first word the second letter of the second word and so on, then mixed them up until I had a recognisable name. 'Ingenious,' he said, 'but wrong.'

# MAENCLOCHOG

The next day we met in Maenclochog. He looked at the chess pieces. He asked me about my father, who had been a builder during the early part of my childhood, before becoming a graphic artist in his middle years. The little man nodded knowingly. 'And your grandmother, his mother, was she from Ireland?'

This time I nodded, open-mouthed, but he didn't explain. I was shocked, enticed, I needed to know! I knew very little about my paternal grandmother. But even though I bombarded him with questions, he said no more about her. How did he know?

The truth was my father's mother had died very young; she was just fifty and contracted typhoid fever from a germ picked up in a swimming pool. Unusually for her time she was very keen on keeping fit and swam every day. My father, who was only nineteen when she died, was devastated by her death. He never spoke about her again.

Of course as we grew, we became fascinated by this mystery woman, but the only knowledge we have of her is what we have gleaned from our mother who knew her briefly. We knew that she originated in Ireland, moved to Chelmsford in Essex, her family were market gardeners and lived in a two-up two-down house and were very poor. My sister and I have tried to search for records of her but so far have drawn a blank.

He took the black rook from the set of chessmen and said it would do nicely. I wondered what my brother would say if he found out that I had allowed one piece of the old and possibly valuable set to be taken? We had both learned to play chess with these pieces. Protest seemed impossible; my companion was desperate to get back home and I seemed to be able to provide some of the items he needed. 'Come, we must hurry,' he said, 'we mustn't be found here.'

We ran and ran until we were out of breath. I didn't know why we were running. When we had got our breath back I asked why. 'It's probably better that you don't know,' he snapped. I remonstrated but could see he would not be budged.

Then we sat down on a bench and he told me about Maenclochog which was a special place. Its name means 'ringing stone', and refers to two large stones next to Ffynnon Fair (Mary's Well). We looked for them and the well but couldn't find them. My friend took me to see a little white cottage that has remained unchanged for over 200 years. It was home to a family of twelve. He placed the herbs that we had collected the previous day under a stone in the garden.

We then continued our journey to Crymych. On the way I volunteered another guess at his name: Htrae Dniw Erif Retaw.

'Clever,' he said. I didn't explain how I arrived at it – he knew – can you guess? It may not be worth your while since it was wrong, but I could tell that he liked it. A clue is that stories need all of these.

# CRYMYCH

We soon arrived in Crymych, high up in the Preseli Hills. This town has a strange, dreamlike character. Does it have something of the Wild West about it? A cattle station high in the hills, where for centuries, farmers, drovers and shepherds have gathered to send their livestock to market, down a pint or two and catch up on the latest tales from the hills. The railway came, and the railway went, and the small hill town carried on. Standing guard over the town are two fine rounded hills – Frenni Fawr and Frenni Fach. You could ask a Welsh speaker to explain those names.

We sat on a wall outside the school, one of the highest in Wales, and my friend told me a dream story from the Mabinogion.

## THE DREAM OF MACSEN WLEDIG

Whilst this tale takes place firstly in Rome and secondly in Caernarfon, much of the hunting takes place in what is now called Pembrokeshire and the Emperor lends his name to Cadair Facsen (The Chair of Macsen). The cairn or burial mound of Frenni Fawr is said to be the place of dreams.

Macsen Wledig, the emperor of Rome, was handsome and wise. He summoned a council of kings and said, 'Tomorrow we will hunt.' So the next day in the morning he set off with his retinue, reaching a river that flowed towards Rome. He hunted through the valley until midday, accompanied by thirty-two crowned kings. It was not for the delight of hunting that the emperor took them, but to put himself on equal terms with them.

The sun was high in the sky overhead, and the heat was very great. Sleep came upon Macsen Wledig. His attendants set their shields on spearshafts to shade him from the sun, and placed a gold enamelled shield under his head; and so Macsen slept. He dreamt, and this is his dream.

He was following the river towards its source, and he came to the highest mountain in the world. The mountain seemed as high as the sky, and when he surmounted it, he seemed to go through the fairest region ever seen, on the far side of the mountain. He saw mighty rivers descending from the mountain to the sea, and he headed towards the source. There, at the mouth of the largest river he'd ever seen, he saw a great city, and a vast castle in the city, and many high coloured towers on the castle. He saw a fleet at the mouth of the river, the largest he'd ever seen. One ship was larger and finer than all the others, with gilded and silvered planks. A whalebone bridge led from the vessel to the land, which he crossed to the ship. Sails were hoisted, and it was borne across the ocean.

He reached what seemed the fairest island in the whole world, and crossed it to the further shore. He saw valleys and cliffs, rocks of wondrous height, and rugged precipices. Facing this rugged land, he saw another island in the sea, and between him and this island was a country with a vast plain and huge mountain. A river flowed through the land and fell into the sea. At its mouth he saw a castle, the fairest ever seen. Its gate was open, and he went inside. He saw a beautiful hall, with a gilded roof, walls inlaid with glittering precious gems, golden doors and seats, and silver tables. Sitting opposite him, two auburn-haired youths played gwyddbwyll, a game like draughts or chess, with a silver board and golden pieces. The youths wore jet-black satin, and their hair was bound in gold, with sparkling precious jewels, rubies, and gems. They had boots of new Cordovan leather, fastened by red gold clasps.

By a pillar he saw a powerful hoary headed man in an ivory chair, carved with golden eagles. He wore gold bracelets, rings on his hands, a golden torque about his neck, and his hair was bound with a golden diadem. In front of him was a gwyllbwyll board and a gold rod, and with a steel file he was carving out gwyddbwyll pieces.

He saw a maiden sitting before the man in a gold chair. She rivalled the sun in beauty. She wore a white silk vest with gold clasps, a cape of gold tissue, and a frontlet of red gold on her head, with rubies, gems and pearls. She was girdled in gold – the fairest sight that man ever beheld.

The beautiful young woman stood as he approached, and introduced herself as Elen. He threw his arms around her neck. They sat down together in the gold chair. He had his arms around the maiden's neck, his cheek by her cheek, but suddenly there was the sound of the chafing of the leashed hunting dogs, the clashing of shields as they struck against each other, the beating of spear shafts, and the neighing and prancing of the horses. The emperor was aroused from his dream.

Rudely awakened, his spirit and existence deserted him. He was filled with love for the dream maiden. Then his companions said, 'Lord, it is time for to take food.' So the emperor mounted his steed, and sadly continued towards Rome.

He stayed like this for a week. When the household went to drink wine from golden vessels, he went with none of them. When they listened to songs and tales, he did not join them. He could be persuaded to do nothing but sleep. When he slept, he dreamt of the maiden he loved best, but when he slept he did not know where in the world she was.

One day the page of the chamber, who was also the King of the Romans, spoke to him. 'Lord, all the people revile you.'

'Why?' asked the emperor.

'Because they get no message or answer from you, as men rightly expect from their lord.'

The emperor said, 'Bring me the wise men of Rome, and I will tell them why I am sorrowful.'

The wise men were brought. 'Sages of Rome, I had a dream in which I beheld a maiden, and because of her I no longer have life, nor spirit, nor existence.'

This was their advice. 'Send messengers for three years to the three continents of the world to search for your dream.'

So the messengers journeyed for a year, wandering about the world, seeking any tidings of his dream. But when they returned at the end of the year, they knew nothing more than the day they set out. Then the emperor was exceedingly sad, thinking he would never have news of she whom he loved best.

Now, the King of the Romans said, 'Go hunting by the route you saw in your dream, whether east or west.' So the emperor went hunting, and reached the bank of a river.

'This is the very place I was when I had the dream. I followed the source of the river westward.'

Thirteen messengers of the emperor set off westwards towards a high mountain which seemed to them to touch the sky. They travelled wearing one sleeve of their cape to the front, showing the world that they were messengers, to keep them from harm in whatever hostile lands they passed. Having crossed the mountain, they saw vast plains, and large rivers.

'Look,' they said, 'see the land which our master saw.' They reached the mouths of the rivers, flowing to the sea, the vast city, and the many coloured high towers on the castle. They saw the largest fleet in the world in the harbour, and the ship that was larger than any of the others.

'Look,' they said, 'here is our master's dream.' In the great galleon they crossed the ocean, and came to the Island of Britain. They crossed the island until they came to Snowdon.

'Behold,' they said, 'the rugged land that our master saw.' They continued until they saw Ynys Môn (Anglesey) spread out before them, and Arfon likewise.

'Behold,' they said again, 'the land our master saw in dreams.' They saw Aber Seiont at Caernarfon, and a castle at the mouth of that river.

The portals of the castle were open, they continued inside and saw the hall in the castle.

'Behold,' they said, 'the hall which he saw in his sleep.' In the hall they saw two youths playing gwyddbwyll on the golden bench. And they saw the hoary headed man in the ivory chair by the pillar, carving playing pieces. And then they beheld the maiden sitting on a golden chair.

The messengers knelt down before her, saying, 'Empress of Rome, all hail !'

'You seem like honourable men,' she said, 'so what is this mockery? My name is Elen.'

'We do not mock you, lady. The Emperor of Rome dreamt of you in his sleep, and because of you he has neither life nor spirit left. We come to ask you to choose, whether to come with us and be made empress of Rome, or that the emperor comes here and takes you for his wife.'

'My lords,' laughed the maiden. 'I will not deny your request, but neither will I believe it too readily. If the emperor truly loves me, let him come here to seek me.'

By day and night the messengers hastened back to Rome. When their horses failed, they bought fresh ones. And when they returned to Rome, they saluted the emperor.

'We will guide you, our lord,' they said, 'over sea and over land, to where the woman is, for we know her name, her kindred, and her place.'

Immediately the emperor set forth with his army, guided by these men, towards the Island of Britain over the sea and the deeps. He conquered the Island from Beli son of Manogan and his sons, and drove them into the sea. Then he proceeded to Arfon, and everywhere he went, the emperor knew the land as soon as he saw it. When he beheld the castle of Aber Seiont he exclaimed, 'Look there, that is the castle where I saw the damsel whom I best love.'

He continued into the castle, into the hall, and there he saw Cynan son of Eudaf, and Adeon son of Eudaf, playing at gwyddbwyll. Then he saw their father Eudaf son of Caradog, sitting on an ivory chair of ivory carving playing pieces. And there was the maiden of whom he had dreamed in his sleep, sitting on a golden chair.

'Empress of Rome,' said he, 'all hail!' And the emperor threw his arms about her neck, and that night she became his bride.

Next morning, the damsel asked for her maiden dowry. He told her to name what she would. She asked to have the Island of Britain for her father, from the North Sea to the Irish Sea, together with the three islands of Môn (Anglesey), Manaw (Man) and Lundy, to hold under the empire of Rome; and to have three chief castles built for her, wherever she chose in the Island of Britain. She chose the chief castle to be at Arfon (Caernarfon), and they brought earth from Rome to Caernarfon so it would be more healthy for the emperor to sleep, sit, and walk upon. The two other castles were built for her at Caerleon and Carmarthen.

One day the emperor went to hunt at Carmarthen, and his chase ranged as far as the top of Frenni Fawr at Crymych in Pembrokeshire. The place the emperor pitched camp that night is still called Cadair Macsen to this day.

Then Elen decided to make high roads from one castle to another throughout the Island of of Britain, and so they were made. For this reason are they called Ffyrdd Elen (Sarn Helen – Helen's causeway), because she was a native of this Island, and the men of the Island of Britain would not have made these great roads for anyone other than Elen. And this dream is called the Dream of Macsen Wledig, emperor of Rome.

That was a tale about Frenni Fawr. Then my friend told a story of its neighbouring hill, Frenni Fach.

## Temptation

A young shepherd boy was tending his father's flock on Frenni Fach mountain just outside Crymych. He sat down to rest and looked at the clouds to see what the weather might bring. It was well known that if the fog fell to the Carmarthenshire side of the mountain it would bring foul weather, whereas if it fell to the Pembrokeshire side it would bring fair. But his gaze was interrupted by a group of soldiers marching by. He was surprised to see them and thought to take a closer look. He climbed on to a rock for a better view. They were not as far away as he had thought at first. Rather they were very small for soldiers. As he came closer he realised that these were the *Tylwyth Teg*. He felt a mixture of fear and fascination. He went closer still – he would be able to tell his family about what he had seen. After all, his cousin had told him that the *Tylwyth Teg* didn't harm anyone who was kind to them.

He managed to hide behind a standing stone, and watched the small people in their dance in a perfect circle. They were dressed in red and white; some were riding on tiny prancing horses. They were so happy that it made him feel a warm glow inside.

One of the fairy folk saw the boy watching them. They all stopped dancing. The boy became scared. They smiled at him and beckoned him. He came out from behind the standing stone and walked slowly towards them. He thought of running away; he'd seen enough to tell his family and friends, he would even be able to bring them here to see the very place where the *Tylwyth Teg* had danced. But they seemed so friendly and smiled and beckoned to him.

He came to the edge of the ring that their dancing had made on the ground, and placed the tip of his toe inside the circle. The most beautiful music immediately filled his ears, making him feel so good that he jumped into the place of their dance. Now he flew through the air, and landed in a beautiful palace, which shone with gold and jewels. He went inside and found it most comfortable; the fairies brought him whatever he desired without him even having to ask. He wanted to stay there forever. The fairies were beautiful to watch, and the music was the most wonderful he had ever heard. The food was more delicious than anything he had eaten before. They even brought him wine which he liked very much. No sooner had he downed the goblet than its contents were magically replenished. He roamed through the palace each day exploring the rooms, the gardens, the boxes and the trunks of treasure.

The one place that he was forbidden was the fountain, in the middle of a lovely garden. He agreed to give the fountain a wide berth, never to touch the coloured fish that swam in the pool beneath it, nor to touch, let alone drink the water.

He was happy enough exploring the rooms and treasures within the palace. When he was hungry food and drink miraculously appeared before him. When he was tired a bed materialised wherever he happened to be. He was happy enough, wasn't he?

The odd thing about mortal humans is that it really doesn't matter how much you have, how many of your desires and thoughts are fulfilled; after a while, the thing you want is the thing you can't have, that thing that has been forbidden. He put it from his mind. He was happy with the music, the food and the beautiful things and beautiful people around him. Wasn't he?

But he couldn't get the thought of the fountain out of his head. The lovely gardens that surrounded it, the beautiful fish that swam in the pool beneath, the tinkling of the water as it splashed into the pool. The more he thought about it the more he wanted to peep at it. Surely just a look wouldn't hurt, would it?

He decided that he would just look. He entered the beautiful garden. The fruits and flowers that grew here were like none he had ever seen before. He explored that garden but didn't touch anything. When his mouth watered and his fingers itched to pick and taste what grew there, he hurried back to the palace, and wished for a bed so that he could snuggle down and sleep and keep away from temptation. He slept, but then woke when the moon was high in the sky. He wondered what the garden would look like in moonlight. Surely just a look wouldn't hurt, would it?

He got out of bed, and a pair of warm slippers materialised beside him. He regarded them as an encouragement. Putting them on, he crept back to the garden. It was more beautiful in the moonlight than he could have imagined. He crept through the garden looking at the fruit and the flowers, marvelling at the sight of them. One particular vine hung with luscious fruit; it was draped down a wall, the moon gave the fruit a beautiful lustre, it was dripping with dew. Surely just a taste of just one of the fruits wouldn't hurt. Would it?

His mouth was dry and the fruit looked moist. He put out his hand, and the vine seemed to lean towards him. He plucked one. He ate it. It was the most delicious fruit he'd ever eaten. He couldn't believe the taste, he had to try another – it was divine – then another just to make sure. He spat the pips on the ground. They seemed to take root straight away. More vines started to grow. He felt better about his greed. More fruit would grow as a result of his gluttony. He crept back through the garden and got back into bed. In the morning when he woke up he rather thought that the smiles on the faces of his attendants were less than wide.

He was embarrassed at his behaviour and determined to keep away from the garden. However, that night he woke again with a burning desire to see the garden again. He got out of bed and found the warm slippers then made his way to the special garden. The vine seemed to have recovered from his feast the night before. It made him feel braver about going to the pool.

He walked slowly towards the pool, looking over his shoulder now and then to make sure he was not observed. It was beautiful; the fish that swam there were of many colours, the water that splashed into the pool from the fountain reflected every colour in the garden. He stood and looked. Looking can't hurt, can it?

He resisted temptation and went back to bed and slept. The next day he was served by fairies with frowns on their faces. But nothing bad happened. The next night he went back. He watched the fish; he looked at the water; he couldn't resist it. He plunged his hand into the water and grabbed a fish.

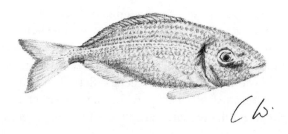

There was a loud scream that reverberated around the garden. The fish disappeared from his hand. The fountain, the pool, the garden and finally the palace melted away and he was left standing in the field where his sheep were grazing.

No matter where he looked or how hard he wished he could never find that place or those people again. No one at home had missed him and none believed his stories about where he'd been. Because he had only been gone a matter of minutes, hadn't he?

I enjoyed this story and knew exactly where to place it in my book. In my determination to find out more about our quest, I asked my friend, 'Could you tell me more about the objects. Are they tokens, or perhaps they act together as a talisman for your journey home?'

The basketful was familiar to me, and of course to any storyteller, or playwright, film-makers, anyone who tells tales. And for weeks now, I had spent all my time helping my friend with his seemingly endless collection, in order to … what? What exactly was the point of all this?

Then a light began to dawn on me. I had been so blinkered. Now I had a revelation. I asked him outright: 'If these objects are not returned by you, does it mean our stories will all die?' He nodded his head very slowly. I was shocked.

He looked sad and tired. He told me that the next day we were to meet by the Tudor Merchants House in Tenby. We needed to add a 'lucky bean' to our collection of objects.

# TENBY, DINBYCH Y PYSGOD

I racked my brains. What was a 'lucky bean'? Like all of the other objects it would have a relevance to the place or a story told here, so the next day I went early to Tenby and spent some time in the museum, looking through archives to see if I could find a clue. The librarian was very helpful, and hunted out several precious tomes. I was instructed to only use pencil in making my notes and told to wear a pair of cotton gloves to avoid damaging anything.

I discovered in some notes on *Pembrokeshire Folk-Lore*, by Bertram Lloyd, that lucky beans were heart-shaped stones, washed up amongst the seaweed and flotsam and jetsam on Pembrokeshire beaches. It is suggested in the set of notes by this gentleman that these 'beans' originate in Mexico.

I walked on the beach searching for one of these special stones, but was unlucky. Time was running out and I hurried along to the Tudor Merchants House. Built in the fifteenth century, this house has authentic Tudor fittings and vividly illustrates Tudor family life.

My companion was already there. I arrived breathless, but he looked down his nose at me and sighed. When I asked him what was wrong he looked sad and said that he hadn't managed to find a 'lucky bean'. He looked even more miserable when I told him that I had also searched the seashore without luck.

But, you know, something was niggling away at the back of my head. I had seen heart-shaped stones, I was racking my brains to remember where. It suddenly came to me! 'Eirian Short,' I said. He looked at me oddly. 'Eirian Short, the artist, had a number of these heart-shaped stones which she had collected and placed in her garden in Dinas, in the north of the county.'

I knew Eirian and would be able to ask her if we could have one. When I first came to live in Pembrokeshire I met Eirian at a gathering of artists. I had been delighted, since as a student of arts in the sixties, I had found her textile work inspiring. She had been a tutor at my art school in London. Now here she was on my doorstep.

I saw that he wasn't really listening as I rambled on. Then when I explained that the stones that I had seen had been painted red to resemble hearts and placed in a heart-shaped garden – he shook his head.

'It has to be here and it can't be altered. The red paint will mean they are not usable.'

I then had a brainwave.

I asked my companion, 'Do you know why it is that everyone all over the world (a slight exaggeration!) knows Pembrokeshire?'

He shrugged, I could tell by his expression that he thought I was wasting valuable time. 'Because they have had a holiday in Tenby!' he replied.

'And why Tenby?' I questioned.

'Because of the sunshine?' he said, getting irritated.

He couldn't understand my excitement and started to look angry, muttering, 'What does this have to do with finding a lucky bean? Time is running out.'

'No it isn't just because of the sunshine here. There are two sandy beaches. We have only looked here on the south beach. There's also the north beach.'

We went there straight away, walked along the tideline and, lo and behold, in amongst the seaweed, there was the very stone my friend sought. His eyes lit up as he picked it up and proudly showed it to me. He couldn't be more delighted if he had found a gold coin. But we won't go there again.

He then took the 'lucky bean' and skimmed it into the sea. I watched as it bounced three times over the surface of the water. I couldn't believe that he would do that after all the trouble we had taken. When I questioned him he said, 'That lucky bean must go on a different journey. I simply had to help it get started.'

The only thing he would say after that was that if I found lucky beans on any beach in the county, I could keep one for luck, but only if I returned all others to the sea by skimming just as he had done.

Then we sat on the beach and he told me a story.

## GREEN GOWN

Two young women sat outside the window of a farmhouse, just outside Tenby. They were chatting and stitching. The two girls were cousins. Agnes was the daughter of the farmer who rented this farm and the surrounding land. The other was the daughter of his brother who now kept a grocer's shop in Haverfordwest. She was called Rose and she had been brought up in the town, unused to the rural way of life.

Agnes explained to her cousin that her father was making hay the next day if the weather stayed fine. Had she ever made hay? Rose said no, but that she had once watched with her mother. She thought that it looked like very hard work.

'Oh, dear that would never do here,' said Agnes.

'We don't allow people to look on. If you come into the field you must work. Besides you may get a green gown.'

Rose asked what it was; her cousin laughed and told her with a twinkle in her eye that she must find out tomorrow. Rose pondered for a while, suspicious that something was afoot. Then she asked Agnes if she thought that they might see William Bowen at the haymaking the next day. Agnes blushed and said that he did come some years, but she wasn't sure if he would come this year. 'Anyway, I don't care if he comes or not!'

Rose thought that this probably meant that Agnes did care very much. She decided to provoke her cousin, who she suspected of planning some mischief for her at the hay making.

'Well,' said Rose, 'I hope he does come because I like him very much!' Agnes stared at her but said nothing then changed the subject.

What Rose didn't know about haymaking was that if a stranger entered a hay field, he or she is seized by the haymakers of the opposite sex and rolled into the hay until a fine is paid or until the others decided that the novice has had enough, hence the term 'green gown'.

The next day was bright and sunny. The cousins proceeded to the hay field. Rose willingly lent a hand, and was pleasantly surprised that haymaking was less strenuous than she had thought. They looked up at a noise on the other side of the hedge. Then William Bowen jumped the hedge and came to meet them. Agnes found her heart was beating fast. She had been rolled in the hay every year by this young man and had a 'green gown' as a result. But he was very shy in her presence this year and she felt very reserved because of her feelings for him.

They exchanged greetings, but William spent more time talking to Rose than to her. Then he initiated her cousin into the ritual of the green gown amidst much laughter. Agnes felt rejected.

Later that day, after milking, they all sat down to tea, but Agnes had lost her appetite. She watched the others laughing and joking and felt miserable. Her eyes filled with tears and she went outside and cried. She felt jealous that 'her' William preferred cousin Rose.

Suddenly she felt an arm encircle her waist. There was William Bowen on his knees beside her. She pretended to reject him, saying why didn't he go back to Rose, since he was so preoccupied with her today. He ignored her coolness. 'I've been waiting all day for a chance to be alone with you.' And he whispered in her ear. She dried her eyes and smiled.

That night William Bowen spoke to her father and he accepted the proposal of marriage for his daughter Agnes.

On her wedding day she wore a gown of green made for her by her mother.

Rose was bridesmaid and caught Agnes' bouquet .

As he shared this tale, the tide began to turn, covering the sands of North Beach. We started to walk towards the harbour. Seeing the Fourcroft Hotel above us on the cliff reminded me of storytelling of a different kind. I thought just this once I would have something to tell that my companion would surely not know.

William Haggar was a fairground film-maker, born in Essex in 1851. He ran away from home at a very young age, and having learnt to play the cornet, got a job as a travelling musician.

At twenty he married Sarah, a member of the fairground 'Inimitable Walton family'. For thirty eight years they travelled the length of England and Wales, 'following the coal', raising eleven children, and entertaining people wherever they went.

Always open to new ideas, Haggar bought a primitive film projector. Those early projectors were quite dangerous, since the film itself was likely to burn and explode. But that was not enough for the inventive showman. He began experimenting with making as well as projecting films. His first effort showed a train arriving at Burry Port station. Audiences apparently screamed in fear as the train approached. Encouraged by this success, Haggar moved on to fiction. He became one of the first movie storytellers, long before Hollywood. With two theatre companies in the family, he had a ready-made cast for his first film: *The Maid of Cefn Ydfa* (Cefn Ydfa means 'back of the wheatfield', the name of the Maid's house).

For the next three years, William made *The Poachers*, *The Sign of the Cross*, *The Life of Charles Peace* and *The Mirthful Mary* series. With more films to show, and more audiences keen to view them, William bought buildings throughout Pembrokeshire and Wales to open as a chain of cinemas. He died a wealthy man.

Today the Fourcroft Hotel has a collection of film memorabilia from the Haggar family, on display in their Hollywood Bar. I turned to look at my companion, who was once again nodding wisely: 'If you ever manage to see one of those films, look carefully at the faces of the extras.' Once again he had beaten me to it. I looked at him in astonishment. I wondered again how old he was.

We walked rapidly now past the harbour, past the old public bath house with its encouraging slogan: 'The Sea Cleanses all Human Wrongs' (written in Greek), and continued until we were opposite St Catherine's Rock, an island at high water. I told my friend that the slogan had become the motto of the town. In return, he recited a story poem by Richard Mason about St Catherine's Rock.

# THE SPECTRE SHIP AND PIRATE CHIEF

*A tale of St Catherine's Rock*

Where Tenby greets the sea, one winter even,
(Three hundred years since then have passed away,)
Across the main by the fierce storm-fiend driven,
A vessel swept along Carmarthen bay;
The waves roared round her in their boisterous play;
The sea-fowls shrieked above her creaking mast;
And, as the shades of night obscured the day,
Fiercer and fiercer grew the raging blast,
The billows rolled more wild, the vessel drove more fast.

No human forms were seen upon her deck,
As she swept onward to the treacherous strand;
No hand was there to guide, no power to check-
Onward she came! But by the little band,
Who watched her as she neared the threat'ning land,
'Twas said that fire-lights danced upon each shroud,
And, ere she sank engulphed within the sand,
Dark spirit-forms were seen her deck to crowd,
And voices not of earth were heard in accents loud.

Th' affrighted landsmen fled, and all the night
Strange sounds were heard above the moaning wind;
But, when they came to gaze at morning light,
No vestige of the vessel could they find.
The storm had lulled, nor left one trace behind;
Only upon the shore was laid, asleep,
A human form, in garments strange confined,
Unwakened by the rippling of the deep,
Or the wild sea-birds' cries that oer him vainly sweep.

And afterwards he would not live with them,
But in the ruins of this lonely rock
Would pass his time, seeking each ocean gem,

Or listening to the wild waves' warring shock,
That vainly at his island home would knock;
Till one, who day by day had seen him there,
While tending in the neighbouring fields his flock,
Missing th' accustom'd form, with kindly care,
Sought the lone isle, and food and covering with him bare.

And (oft he told the tale) he found him sitting
Upon a crag, while ocean laved his feet,
With the wild sea-birds round him, o'er him flitting,
Scared by his presence from their wonted seat;
That, having found him in this rude retreat,
He offered food and help, and urged him leave
So lone a spot, and come to home more meet;
That he his words did courteously receive,
But said to leave that isle would make him ever grieve.

But then he told him of his former life,
How he had been a pirate on the sea,
Told him of many a scene of blood and strife,
And spoke beside of love, and how that he
Had slain in some strong fit of jealousy,
Though innocent, the one who loved him most.
How all his comrades perished fearfully,
And how his bark, all strained and tempest-tost,
Was manned by spirit forms, and wrecked upon that coast.

'And now at times,' he said, 'sea maidens come,
And beckon me to yonder ocean's breast;
Last night they came and called me to their home,
And told me she was happy and at rest;-
And – see! 'tis she! Upon that billow's crest!'
He pointed to a white wave rolling on:
'I come! I come! Receive me, spirits blest!'
He said, and sprang; the ocean wave came rolling on,
The shepherd saw no more, but went, and went alone.

And so he died! And men in after times
Wept as they pondered o'er his dark career,
Pitied his faults, and half excused his crimes,
With none to solace, and few to cheer;
And though there were who shed a sorrowing tear
In pity for his fate, yet even those
Were not allowed to soothe his sufferings here;
Alone, untended, in life's dreadful close,
His spirit fled to seek – we trust to find – repose.

His recitation brought the poem, and the story it contained, to life. I smiled.

The following day's port of call was Manorbier, there was no token. My friend wanted to read an inscription in the graveyard of St James' Church. I eagerly looked forward to this part of our journey. Manorbier had been described by Giraldus Cambrensis as 'the pleasantest spot in Wales'. He may have been a little biased because that was where he was born, in the twelfth century.

# MANORBIER

We met by the castle, which has been well-preserved, with magnificent views out to sea. I could see what Gerald of Wales was getting at and I made a mental note to return sometime to explore at leisure. My companion pointed towards the nearby church. We made our way there and he asked me to wait by the clocktower and not to peep.

I did as bidden but felt rather excluded. I would rather have explored the castle than stood there cooling my heels.

Returning from the church, my friend saw that I looked rather fed up and suggested we sit down and share a story. He started.

## CUSTOMS AND EXCISE

In 1825, in Swanlake, there was a shopkeeper called John James. He and his wife Nancy ran an ironmongers and lived above the shop.

One night Nancy was awakened by grunts, footsteps and the sound of cartwheels on the road outside. She turned over to wake her husband. He was not in bed beside her. She got up, lit the candle, pulled on a shawl and went to the window. There was a cart outside, and men were unloading barrels into the shop.

She crept quietly down the stairs, blew out the candle and sat on the stairs to watch and listen. There was her husband showing the men down to the cellar. She watched many barrels carried down.

Because of the hour and the secrecy with which the goods were being stored, it was not hard to guess that the goods were stolen. She had always wondered if her husband dabbled in a bit of smuggling, as many other locals did. But she was angry, feeling that she should at least have been told. She crept back to bed, but didn't sleep much that night.

Next morning she waited for an explanation from her husband. Eventually she confronted him with what she had seen. Shamefacedly, he admitted that he was temporarily storing smuggled goods in their cellar. She was furious! When her husband went to the ale house she went downstairs and counted the barrels. Then she set off to report the matter to the Customs officials anticipating a handsome reward – probably in the region of £200.

Going through Manorbier she stopped off at a friend's house, to confide what she was about. When she continued on her journey, the 'friend' quickly rushed to the ale house to tell John James. He gathered together his fellow smugglers, and together cleared the house within an hour or so. Now the goods were concealed in a well at nearby Manorbier Castle.

When the wife arrived back with a smug expression and a band of Customs men, she was rather put out and embarrassed to find the cellar was returned to its normal state and cleared of contraband. The Customs men set off without another word, guessing that the row in this house would continue for some time – and it did. Nancy never again spoke to the so-called 'friend' who she guessed had informed on her.

I said I had another smugglers story from this coast. My friend said, 'you will never run out of smuggling tales around here.'

## CAPTAIN JACK FURZE

In around 1800 Captain Jack Furze took the farm that was being let on the estate of Manorbier Castle. Local people found him to be jolly and friendly. He amused his neighbours with yarns of the sea. Now he had saved a little money, he intended farming the land, and digging for coal on the farm. But he kept his hand in by keeping a small brig, the *Jane*.

What locals didn't realise at first was that Jolly Jack Furze was using the mining and farming activities as a front for smuggling. In addition, he was using the castle cellars for storing his ill-gotten gains.

It all came out one day when Jack's ship, the *Jane*, was heading for the coast and one of the King's ships appeared on the horizon. The winds were with the King's vessel and she came close to the *Jane*, firing shots and making the small craft reel. Captain Jack ordered his crew to pull the ship round and use the wind to take her away. Being a smaller craft, with the wind in her sails, she made good speed. The chase went on for an hour.

But as the sun sunk low in the sky, the King's ship gained on them. More shots were fired. Captain Jack commanded his men to go below decks. He took the helm himself while shots continued to cut up his rigging and destroy the decking. When darkness finally came the King's ship, fearful of the rocky coast, drew away. Captain Jack was reported to have said, 'I told you so, the timber is not spliced that'll run down Jack Furze!'

Locals did say that the incident was too close for comfort, and having had enough fun for the time being, Captain Jack settled back to a quiet life of farming and mining. Believe that if you like!

The next day we were to meet at Pembroke. The object was a fleece. I explained that I may be able to help. Some time ago I had thoughts of taking up spinning. A friend had given me a fleece to make a start. It was at about that time that I was approached to write this book, so now the fleece was gathering dust in a corner of my studio. Spinning was for another day.

He agreed without much enthusiasm that I could bring it, and asked if I had any more thoughts about his name. I had been racking my brains but it had not yet come to me. I asked if he would humour me and play the game we used to play as children, when we played hide-and-seek. Coming close to what was sought, the person who had hidden the thimble or other object said: warm; warmer; hot; burning; on fire. Or, alternatively: cool; colder; freezing; and ice. He was amused and nodded.

# PEMBROKE, PENFRO

It was midday in Pembroke, and raining. I stood outside the town hall with my umbrella, but it was so windy that it turned inside out. In my rucksack was the fleece. The little man was late. This was new. He had never been late before. I began to worry and realised that I was getting quite fond of him, despite his grumpy demeanour.

I threw the ruined umbrella in the nearest bin and when I returned, he was waiting at the appointed spot. He asked me why I was late. I was speechless! We went to a small café. I showed him the fleece and he was pleased and said it would do. He then placed it around his shoulders explaining that it wasn't one of the tokens, but he needed an extra layer as the evenings were chilly. I asked where he was staying, his reply was evasive. 'Here and there,' he said.

He quickly changed the subject by telling me a story about Princess Nest, and then another about a friend of his who frequently disguised himself as a weasel.

## PRINCESS NEST (CAPTIVATING BEAUTY)

Almost 1,000 years ago a daughter was born to Prince Rhys ap Tewdwr, who ruled Deheubarth (the ancient kingdom that absorbed Pembrokeshire). She was called Nest. When she was just thirteen her father was killed in battle and she was taken hostage by King William II of England, known as William Rufus. Nest was taken out of Wales and brought to the royal court.

As she approached womanhood, she became a great beauty. Bards wrote songs about her; poets wrote about her loveliness. The King's younger brother Henry fell in love with her. She bore him a son, one of many illegitimate children.

King William died — perhaps murdered, we don't know for sure. Henry became King – the first of eight Henrys – and was pressed to marry for political reasons. Monarchs rarely married for love, and Nest was neither useful nor powerful enough to be made his wife. So Henry married her off to one of his trusted followers,

Gerald de Windsor, the Constable of Pembroke. The newlyweds went to live in Cilgerran Castle.

Gerald was delighted to be married to the most sought-after woman in Wales. She was not only beautiful, but clever and funny. He could not believe his luck. But it was not all plain sailing, as he was continually challenged to keep his warriors in order. One by one they all fell in love with her. Gerald and Nest were content enough, they had five children. All remained well until Owain ap Cadwgan, Nest's second cousin, having heard of her great beauty, paid a visit to see her for himself. Inevitably, Owain fell in love with Nest, and made plans to kidnap her.

Warned that her cousin was planning something, Nest took some precautions. Owain and his men tunneled into Cilgerran Castle, under cover of darkness, set fire to part of the castle, and then sounded the alarm. Their plan was to kill Gerald when he came out of his room to order his men to deal with the fire. But Nest, suspecting treachery, led Gerald to the privy which adjoined the chamber. There, he escaped by way of the privy hole down the garderobe (the lavatory chute) that opened straight from their bedroom down the castle side into the woodland below. She had already hung a rope so that he could climb down and make his escape. It was not the most dignified of exits, but at least he escaped with his life.

Owain carried Nest off into the night. She remained captive for more than two years. King Henry was furious when he heard of the abduction, and civil war ensued. Eventually Owain was defeated in battle and escaped to Ireland. Nest was duly returned to Gerald. Owain was ordered by the King to return from Ireland to Wales. When Gerald was informed of Owain's whereabouts he set an ambush for him and killed him.

Some say that Nest became infatuated with Owain, and that she hatched the escape plan for Gerald to protect her husband from sure death, and to enable her to conduct an affair with Owain under cover of the abduction story. That kept open the option to return to her husband once the affair was over. Others have suggested that she fell in love with Owain only after her capture.

Nest had nine children from four different fathers in the various kidnaps and affairs. You can decide for yourself.

## WEASELS

There was once a person residing at the castle of Penbroch (Pembroke) who found a brood of young weasels concealed within a fleece in his dwelling house. He carefully removed and hid the skin and its contents. The mother weasel, distraught at the loss of her young, and suspecting the householder of killing them, went to a vessel of milk that had been set on the table for the master's young son. Raising herself up, she polluted the milk with her deadly poison, intending the destruction of the child. The man observed what passed and so returned the fleece and its contents. The weasel, now full of maternal feeling, regretted her previous action and so returned quickly to the vessel and overthrew it in gratitude for the recovery of her own offspring, saving the child from danger.

On the way home a weasel ran across the road in front of me.

The next day we would be in Pembroke Dock. I was told not to be late and that the object was a ship in a bottle. This was not just any old ship in a bottle, but must be a wooden-hulled, ninety-gun warship.

It was not going to be easy. That evening I was not able to write. I contacted friends in the search for the ship in the bottle, but none could help. I nearly gave up, but decided to go for a stroll to clear my head. My walk took me past a nearby pub, where I stopped for a glass of wine. There I bumped into Graham and Paul, who before retiring, owned an antique shop. I told them a little of the story and of my quest for a ship in a bottle. Paul told me that they had quite a collection at home, left over from the closing of the business. Some things just could not be sold. Ships in bottles were unfashionable and so most of them had ended up in their home. I was invited to come and look.

The glass case containing the ships in bottles collection was quite incongruous in their lovely house with beautiful works of art adorning the walls. But there, of course, was the very thing I sought, in the case. I asked if I could have it. They looked at each other; old habits die hard. I was told that it would break up the collection and that if I wanted one, I would have to take the lot. This whole adventure was escalating out of control. I agreed a price and walked back home to get my car and my cheque book so that I could take the glass case home with its collection.

When I returned, Graham and Paul were standing outside their house grinning. They helped to load the case on board, then refused any payment. It amused them to think that they still had the gift of bargaining, but were glad to see the back of the collection. It was a dubious privilege. Where as I going to put this case and its contents? For now it went in the shed. The ninety-gun ship in its bottle came into the house ready for the following day. It struck me that I had a collection which I didn't really want, which was now even more unsaleable by the removal of one item.

The next day the beaming look on my friend's face was worth the effort and disruption at home. He danced with joy when I gave him the ship in the bottle. He looked blankly at me when I asked if he would like the rest of the collection.

Clearly not.

# PEMBROKE DOCK,
# DOC PENFRO

We sat down on a seat outside the library and he told me a tale about this very special town with its history of shipbuilding that has shaped the lives of the community for centuries.

# BETTY FOGGY

In Pembroke Dock in the 1850s, there lived a woman called Betty Foggy. She was considered by some to have special powers; by others to be a witch, a caster of spells.

On 21 July 1853 a wooden-hulled, ninety-gun warship, the *Caesar*, was due to be launched. It was customary at that time for the dockyard gates to be opened to the townspeople to enjoy and share in a launch.

The town band was ready, and people were crowding around the dockyard gates waiting for them to be opened.

The policeman on the gate spotted Betty Foggy in the crowd. He knew of her reputation and turned her away, saying that she would throw a shadow of bad luck on the ceremony. Dozens of people watched as she was refused entry. She had a furious look on her face, and some heard her curse out loud as she left. 'If I cannot come in, there will be no launch today.'

The appointed hour arrived, the mayor gave a long speech, the head of the dockyard gave a longer speech, and the band struck up. The new ship started to move down the slipway, then stopped and became stuck fast. The mayor and dignitaries flushed and looked flustered. From their place on the platform they sent for the dockyard manager. The band repeated their repertoire of tunes.

The crowd started murmuring, some people started shouting, and the ship was stuck fast! The curse of Betty Foggy was whispered, then shouted. After much discussion, pointed fingers and red faces, the launch ceremony was cancelled. No refreshments were served, and with much booing, mocking and shouting, the crowd was sent home.

The slipway was rebuilt. The official explanation was that poor quality softwood had been used in its original construction. And just to be on the safe side, a shamefaced dockyard manager quietly called at a small terraced house to make an apology to Betty Foggy. Many people whispered that the successful launch, accompanied by a low-key ceremony a few weeks later, was the result of the curse being lifted by Betty Foggy.

Needless to say she was never turned away from the dockyard gates again. Following this incident, her advice was apparently sought on the suitability of future launch dates. The over-zealous policeman on the gates who had turned her away was deployed on other duties. Many people in the town said: 'We could have told you so.'

I told my friend the story of two smugglers from hereabouts whose stories I had uncovered in my research.

## KING OF SMUGGLERS

William Truscott had been known for many years as 'The King of the Smugglers'. He sailed the seas around the Pembrokeshire Coast, gathering booty from ships or washed ashore on the beach after a storm. This enabled him to dodge customs men and the payment of duty. Many of his ill-gotten gains found their way onto the black market locally. People mostly kept quiet and took advantage of goods sold free of taxes and duty.

Except on one day when someone must have reported him. The Customs men laid in wait near a cave at New Quay near St Govan's, which he used for storage. They arrested him in the act of hiding contraband.

Truscott managed to escape and fled to the Pembroke River. When he tried to cross the water from Bentlas to Pembroke Dock, he was shot and badly wounded by the Customs men, and drowned in the Pembroke River.

The case aroused more than the usual amount of interest, because it appeared that the revenue officer who fired at Truscott did so without warning, and that the officers ignored the injured man's cries for help. The jury at the inquest judged that the conduct of the king's men 'was highly reprehensible, cowardly and cruel'.

## GHOSTS ON BOARD

A new captain had just been appointed to the survey vessel HMS *Asp*. One evening, hearing raised voices coming from his cabin, he rushed to investigate. There was no one there. This happened on a number of occasions without explanation.

Some days later one of the crew reported that the figure of a woman was seen standing on one of the ship's paddle boxes, pointing to the heavens. It was usual to blame the over-consumption of rum when such matters were reported. The apparition made several other appearances, and many crew members refused to be alone on deck.

The vessel put into the Royal Naval yard at Pembroke Dock for repairs. Someone on the quayside saw the same woman and called the guard. They watched her come down the gangplank and walk towards them. The guard challenged her. When she did not respond he levelled his rifle and bayonet at her. The woman walked right through him and disappeared into the night. She was never seen again.

After the stories my companion asked me to take him to the Dockyard Wall to see the bronze panels portraying the history of the town, which had been created by sculptor Perryn Butler.

# ST GOVAN'S

Our next meeting was to be at the little stone chapel at St Govan's. This was the far south of Pembrokeshire, as far as we could possibly be from Pen Cemaes in the north. Somewhere amongst the rocks and pebbles below the chapel in this rocky headland, the object would be found. I was told not to trouble myself to do anything but carry the basket. I arrived at the top of the cliff, alarmed to see the steep steps down to the chapel. There was no sign of the man, but there on the cliff path was the basket full of our treasures. I picked it up, and carefully climbed down the cliff steps, trying to keep my balance with one hand, carry the basket with the other, and keep count of the steps. I reached the chapel wedged tightly between the cliffs, put the heavy basket down on the chapel floor and looked around. Still no sign of the man. I looked further down the rocks, and there he was, near the crashing waves, looking very smug. He saw me, and quickly climbed up to the chapel and handed me a large shell. It rang clear as a bell when hit with a stone. He told me the story of this place and the bell.

## St Govan

Govan, some say Gawain, was walking the southernmost tip of the county when he was set upon by pirates from Lundy Island. Legend has it that a cleft in the rock at what is now called St Govan's Point opened miraculously for Govan to hide in, closed over him, and opened miraculously for a second time after the pirates had gone away. Govan stayed in that cell, drinking water from the sacred well nearby and eating fish. He would toll a silver bell as a warning to others each time the pirates returned. The pirates were not best pleased and stole the bell, but spirits from the sea took the bell from the pirates and returned it to the hermit. To prevent its future theft they encased the bell in a huge stone, The Bell Rock, which can be seen to this day. It is said that when the bell rings, its sound is a thousand times stronger than before. It is possible to see the cave, and legend has it that if you make a wish while standing in the cleft in the rock it will come true, but only if you don't change your mind before you turn around. Take care, the treads have been roughly hewn from the rock. If you count the steps on the way down they do not tally with the number of steps on the way back up.

I put the shell in the basket, which was now even heavier, picked it up, and started climbing back up the steps. Naturally I lost count. At the top I paused to catch my breath. There was the man again, waiting for me. It was hard to say whether I was more puzzled or irritated. Did he really need me to carry the basket all the way down and then back up? But I simply asked him if I was getting warmer with Govan or Bell or Shell, or Cell. 'Freezing,' was his reply.

I told him something I knew about a place near here.

# CASTLEMARTIN

A woman in Castlemartin had once told me of a cure for warts. There are those who should not read this because many have an aversion to these creatures: Black slugs rubbed on warts will cure the condition. Brown slugs are useless.

The following day we were to meet in Monkton. 'What is changing hands?' I asked.

'I have to pay a visit there,' he said

# MONKTON

The appointed place was by the cattle grid at Catshole Quarry, now renamed Castle Quarry. I asked him about the proposed visit. 'Oh, I have already paid my respects.' he said and as we walked through Monkton, past the school, my friend raised his hat.

'Why do you salute the school?'

'Not the school,' he said, 'but the many people who have travelled here through the centuries.' He told me about some of the traditions of the travellers who had settled hereabouts.

## THE WOOD FAMILY

Abram Wood was revered as the King of the Gypsies. He was born before the end of the seventeenth century. His descendants include many musicians who have helped to keep alive musical traditions that were forced underground during the Methodist revival.

One member of this family was appointed chief harpist to Queen Victoria. Another was a teacher of the traditional harp, whose pupils included Nansi Richards, the famous traditional Welsh harpist.

Abram Wood is credited with keeping the Romani language intact 'in the fastnesses of Cambria'. The Wood family was reputed to be fluent in three languages: Romani, English and Welsh.

I told him that the museum in Haverfordwest had worked with the Gypsy unit in the school to recreate a 'Varda' or Gypsy Caravan. He had of course heard about it before.

Tomorrow we would meet in Solva. I should look for a picture of a lighthouse. Before we parted I had another guess at the man's name. 'Hans Shipchess' was an amalgamation of the names of some of the objects which had been removed from collections, like the handkerchief, the ship in the bottle and the chess piece. He shook his head. 'Cold,' he said. I was disappointed.

On the way home I called at the bookshop in Fishguard and found several postcards with pictures of lighthouses. Indeed the bookshop gave out bookmarks with a picture of a lighthouse. It was the symbol for their shop. Barbara and Bridget who owned the bookshop helped me to seek out prints of lighthouses and told me some lighthouse tales. I bought some postcards and they let me borrow some of the prints.

They shared these stories.

## Message in a Bottle

The Smalls Lighthouse has many stories attached to it. I was told that when the designer of the lighthouse, Mr Whiteside, was supervising repairs at the lighthouse, he and the repair workers became stranded and needed supplies. They apparently sent a message in a bottle which – months later – resulted in their rescue, once the bottle had been found many miles away and the finder had sent help.

## Looking After the Light

Thomas Howell and Thomas Griffith were a two-man team looking after the light at the Smalls Lighthouse. Griffith died in a freak accident. Howell was afraid to give the body a sea burial as he feared being accused of murder. Because he was destined to be here some time before the relief crew came, and because he didn't want to keep the body inside, he built a makeshift coffin and lashed it to a ledge on the outside of the lighthouse.

The storms and wild winds lashed the ledge and started to break up the box. The corpse's arm fell through the broken side of the coffin and seemed to be waving at Howell. The poor man was terrified and it was as much as he could manage to keep the lamp lit. When the relief vessel finally landed at the lighthouse and he was finally relieved of duty, he was almost unrecognisable. He was never able to work again, and sat rocking backwards and forwards in his chair looking through the window of his cottage, refusing all food until he eventually passed away.

After this incident, all British lighthouses were always crewed by three keepers.

# SOLFACH, SOLVA

We met outside the Harbour Inn. I presented the postcards and prints of lighthouses. He looked at each one in turn but he shook his head. None of them was right.

I suggested that we visit the art gallery in Solva where a local artist displayed his work. We climbed the steps to the gallery, which was in a converted chapel, searched inside but although there were some pictures of lighthouses, none were what was required. The artist was in the gallery and my friend borrowed my sketchbook and drew what he wanted, then showed the sketch to the artist. I was amazed. The artist was from Cuba and his first language was Spanish, yet my companion seemed fluent and was able to converse freely with him. He was invited into the studio in the next room. They closed the door, leaving me waiting in the gallery. The artist painted a small picture of a lighthouse in flamboyant colours whilst my friend watched and waited. It was pronounced 'just right'. My friend walked away, and I was left to pay.

When I caught him up by the harbour, we sat on the benches outside the inn. I told my companion an anecdote that I had heard about this area.

## BIRD OMEN

In a house in Solva, the housekeeper had been very disturbed by a grey wagtail which had fluttered against the windows of the house, and against the house next door. She was very superstitious and was much troubled and she begged her employer to shoot the bird.

He laughed and said that the bird had probably lost its mate and mistook its own reflection for another grey wagtail. He refused to shoot the bird and the housekeeper said that this would mean a death in the family, and probably one next door as well.

Soon afterwards both households suffered a death in the family.

My companion told me some other things about this area.

## SMUGGLING

It was common knowledge in the old days that the villages around St Bride's Bay were involved in 'the free-trade'. The islands of Skomer and Skokholm to the south were said to be used as smuggling depots.

The *Pelham Cutter*, a ship in service of the customs men, was attacked by two large smuggling ships and a wherry whilst carrying a cargo of goods which were contraband and had been confiscated. The officers on board had to leave the Pelham Cutter and it was boarded by the crew of the wherry. Despite a large reward being offered, none of the cargo was ever returned. The *Cutter* sank to the bottom of the sea just off St David's. The offenders were never convicted.

I told my friend that I had heard there were many houses in Solva with concealed cupboards and shafts that were once used to hide pirated goods.

I had also heard other snippets of stories. Here are some of them.

## WAXING LYRICAL

One particular evening, many years ago, the chapel, which was lit by candles, was visited by excise men who removed all the candles, leaving the congregation in the dark and muttering about smuggled tallow.

At around that time fish were preserved in salt, so this mineral was of great value to fishermen. The tax on salt made it an expensive business and so smuggling of this commodity became quite an industry. Smugglers were able to undercut the selling price of salt. Most of the trading went on at night and, frequently, low price liquor was sold by the same traders.

One day a spy informed the magistrate that a vessel had just come in and that they had salt smuggled aboard. The justice privately sympathised with the smugglers and was anxious not to convict them in this case. So he came very slowly over the hill, roaring like a lion. He shouted that he would punish the smugglers for thieving from his majesty. He was so slow and so loud that the smugglers were able to dispose of the salt. When the customs men boarded the ship no salt was found. It was reported however that the water in Solva Harbour was much saltier than usual that night.

My companion now told me about 'Williet'.


## A SEER AND HIS PROPHECIES

There was one William Howell, locally called 'Williet', who lived just outside Solva in a hamlet called Caerfarchell. He was known locally as a Seer. He was once walking past the workshop of a carpenter. Two brothers and their father were busy repairing the handles of tools for a smallholder.

When Williet saw them he called out that this was mean work for such craftsmen, but not to worry because they would soon be called upon to make a coffin for a man who lived between Solva and St David's. The two brothers were sceptical and laughed at the old man. 'You will believe it,' said Williet, 'because you and your brother will carry the coffin past the 'doctor's' house in Nine Wells.'

Several weeks went by and no death, nor even anyone being ill was reported.

Suddenly one day a messenger came running into the carpenter's workshop, with the news that the crew of one of the small vessels from Solva harbour had gone down in Nolton Haven, ten miles away. One body was brought home in a cart and the carpenters were asked to build a coffin. The two brothers set to work straight away, resolving that they would not be the ones to carry the coffin past the 'Doctor's' house. But it was heavy and needed four carriers. So the Seer's prophecy came true. The brothers were careful to respect Williet after that.

I asked the man if there was much left on the list. Some nights I had been too busy looking for items or trying to fathom out his name, to catch up on my writing. In addition, I was spending quite a lot of money and was worried about running low on funds. He told me that we had nearly assembled everything he needed and, glory be, he thanked me!

Tomorrow's adventure would be in Wolf's Castle. We had been making quite a large circuit of the county. I wondered if we were finally approaching the starting place and completing the circle. We were to meet at the Wolf's camp, which is what local people call the rock formation at the top of the gorge, above the aptly named village of Wolf's Castle. Nothing was required from me apart from carrying the basket.

# CASBLAIDD, WOLF'S CASTLE

We met at the bottom of the hill. I had a rucksack with water and sandwiches, and I was given the basket to carry. It was quite a climb. At the top we sat near the 'Wolf' and had some water and a sandwich. I told my friend, 'The rocks up here look for all the world as if they had been strewn by giants from a great height.'

'I think they look like a bad set of teeth,' he said. We both laughed. Some walkers came by and shook their heads, muttering something about disturbing the tranquility.

We watched a buzzard soaring and swooping down on some unsuspecting crows. They rose up into the air shrieking. 'Tranquility?' my friend laughed again. Afterwards he told me about this special place.

## THE WOLF AND THE LION

It is recorded that the name Wolf was sometimes given to outlaws. Indeed the surrounding valley with beech, ash and chestnut trees did have a reputation as a hiding place for those beyond the law. The roar of the River Anghof has been likened to the roar of a wild animal. Have wolves or lions ever been seen here? Local people have reported sight of the recumbent form of a lion at the top of the steep hill.

The name of the nearby village of Spittal suggests a place of refuge, which may have been a place for the sick or infectious, but could also have been a place of shelter from wolves for the traveller in ancient times.

Wolf's Castle is one of a chain of fortresses along the Landsker Line, built by Anglo Normans to protect their South Pembrokeshire colony.

## OWAIN GLYNDŴR

Owain Glyndŵr was born in the nearby village of Treffgarne, where his mother's family were landowners. His family also had lands in Powys. He was sent to England to be educated, but after his marriage to the daughter of Sir David Hanmer, a distinguished lawyer who had served under Edward III and Richard II, he returned to his lands in Powys.

He was very special to the whole of Wales; a Marcher Lord descended from the Princes of Powys and Cyfeiliog, and on his mother's side, descended from the Prince of Deheubarth (Pembrokeshire.) He held the lordships of Glyn Dyfrdwy and Cynllaith Owain. He was an heir to Cadwaladr.

In mediaeval Welsh folklore there is a prophecy about the rising up of the red dragon. Some people thought that perhaps Glyndŵr would be the dragon.

During the years that followed his return to Wales, the English had firm control over the whole of Wales, insinuating English law into Welsh culture. Owain Glyndŵr's neighbour Reginald de Grey became part of this stranglehold and stole common land. Glyndŵr could get no justice from the king or parliament and, after a long-running dispute over the land, the two fought. The fight became a battle, the battle gathered many followers and then turned into a rebellion. At this time Owain Glyndŵr's followers declared him Prince of Wales. Many punishments were handed out by the English, but the acts of rebellion escalated. Conwy Castle was taken back from the English and many other small battles resulted in the recapture of some lands by the Welsh. Was this the rising up of the red dragon?

Owain Glyndŵr was now in control of most of Wales. There was an immediate response from Oxford, where Welsh scholars dropped their books and flocked home. Welsh labourers in England downed their tools and headed for home.

The English retaliated and their parliament rushed ferocious anti-Welsh legislation on to the statutes. Henry IV marched a big

army across north Wales, burning and looting without mercy. The English started to win back not only their own lands, but captured parts of Wales once more.

Glyndŵr retreated; some of his followers returned to their families and gradually his force was reduced to a small band of loyal followers on the run. He came back to the place of his birth to spend his last years as a fugitive in the fields and valleys of Wolf's Castle. Owain Glyndŵr was a Welsh prince who was never betrayed by his own people, not even in the darkest days when many of them could have saved their lands farms and families by doing so.

Wolf's Castle is said to be his last resting place. In the transformation that happens in all good Welsh tales, the dragon turned into a lion and, finally, a wolf. If you go to Wolf's Castle today you will see, on the top of the gorge the recumbent form of a lion and close by, a wolf forever howling at the moon.

I had always been fascinated by the rock formation and was pleased to hear tales about it. The previous night I had researched Wolf's Castle and I told my companion some stories that I had discovered.

## The Fiery Wagon

In the 1740s, Sarah Bevan of Treffgarne had a vision of 'a line of wagons racing down the centre of the Gorge, suspended above the river, the front wagon appearing from the smoke and flames to be on fire'. Sixty years later the first railway steam engine was invented, and not so long after that a network of railways brought a steam locomotive close by that very place.

## The Tunnel to St David's

On the southern side of Great Treffgarne Mountain is a small cave. It has been said that this is the entrance to a network of tunnels that leads as far as St David's, some twelve miles away. One day many years ago a woman was walking her dog nearby. She let the dog off its lead for a run, and the dog disappeared. The dog disappeared so suddenly that the woman was distraught. She called and whistled until her throat was hoarse. She ran for help. Friends and family came to join in the hunt, but the dog was nowhere to be found. There was nothing else to do but sadly decide that the dog was lost.

The woman and her family returned home, tearfully hung the dog's lead on the back of the door, and the family rallied round to try to help. But she was inconsolable. They put up posters and handed out leaflets describing the missing dog.

Several days later, a woman sweeping her floor in St David's heard a loud scratching and whimpering under the hearthstone. She was afraid and called her husband and son. They listened and heard the disturbance. They lifted the hearthstone and a very thin, hungry, scrawny dog crept out.

Eventually the dog was reunited with his owner in Treffgarne twelve miles away. She was overjoyed, and the story was told in all the pubs and inns, but no-one has ever found the tunnel.

## THE ELEPHANT

There was a travelling circus making its way through west Wales. One of the heavy circus wagons was being hauled up the steep and winding old road through Wolf's Castle. People came out of their houses to see their first elephant and the brightly coloured wagons of the circus. At the top of the hill the poor creature keeled over. Onlookers thought he was dead, but it seemed that he had suffered a heart attack. The local people cared for him, and eventually he became fit to continue his journey.

He only made it to the next village and there in Letterston, he came to rest for the last time.

My friend said, 'it was a sad thing that in the recent past animals were brought away from their homes and trundled around unfamiliar and alien places.'

'Yes,' I agreed, 'but some people in times past would never have seen exotic animals other than in zoos or at the circus.'

On the way back down the hill my companion asked me about Llanwnda and the story of the mermaid from there. 'Don't we have enough mermaid hairs?' I asked. He reminded me that we were still short of one hair. We agreed to meet by the gates of the churchyard.

# LLANWNDA

Next to the church where we met was an artist's studio and home. He was well-known locally as a creator of artworks using recycled materials and a proponent of alternative energy. My friend was more interested in the artist's collection of vehicles, all brightly decorated and adorned with small toy and replica cars, looking like the jewels on a gown.

We went into the gallery and looked at the artworks, helped ourselves to a cup of tea from the kettle, cups, tea and milk kindly left there for passers-by. Then we sat down and my companion told me a tale, which is often repeated locally.

## MERMAID'S ADVICE

A mermaid was said to have been caught by three brothers below Llanwnda, near the spot where the French made their landing many years later. They carried her to their home, and kept her locked away in a secure place for some time. She begged to be allowed to return to the brine land, and said if they returned her she would give them three valuable pieces of advice.

The truth was that her constant wailing disturbed the sleep of every member of the household. She was of no use to them and other members of the family insisted that she was returned.

As they carried her towards the sea she gave the people of the house three pieces of advice; 'Skim the surface of the pottage before adding sweet milk to it: it will be whiter and sweeter, and less of it will do. Take your coins and turn them every time there is a full moon, preferably in the light of the moon. Save some of your cider to pour on the apple tree soon after Hen Galan.'

I am told the family follows the three advices to this day.

As we left the artist's studio, my friend walked along the garden path which led to a cottage nearby. I watched open-mouthed as he posted the picture of the lighthouse through the letter box. I had paid the artist dearly for that picture and now it was just pushed through someone's letter box. This man really was the end. Just in time, I saw that he had scribbled a message on the reverse. Sadly I was not near enough to read it.

He saw I was looking with disapproval, and gave me a look which said "Don't ask".

## JEMIMA NICHOLAS

The French landed at Carregwastad in a remote corner of the Pencaer peninsula, west of Fishguard, in the year 1797. They made free with the homes and possessions of the inhabitants for some time. Through excess of food and drink the soldiers became unruly. A group of women, led by Jemima Nicholas, kept them at bay whilst waiting for soldiers led by Earl Cawdor to arrest them. Their commander, finding it impossible to control his men, surrendered to the local forces.

I asked my friend if he had seen the tapestry in the Town Hall in Fishguard which depicted the story of the landing and which had been made by local people. He said he had not seen it and did not know that it had been placed in the town hall. (Was this a first?)

We searched and searched for the last mermaid hair. It started to get dark, and I fetched a torch from my car. We looked around the pathway and under stones. There was a large piece of quartz embedded in the hedgebank. My companion asked me to lift it. I prised it out and found a hair of silvery hue with a greenish tinge.

We wrapped it carefully and my friend placed it inside his hat with the first two hairs.

We looked at the contents of the basket; he checked his list and nodded. I noticed that the remaining loaf of bread was no longer there. Perhaps that had been for him rather than the collection. He pronounced that everything was there. I asked if we needed to go to Pen Cemaes in order for him to get home. He shook his head. "No it has to be one of the other entrances and it must be tomorrow". He knew now that it was not Narberth so we should try Cwm Cych. We agreed to meet there at midday on the next day and would keep our fingers crossed that it was the right portal.

He said I clearly needed some help with his name, and gave me a riddle. 'My name means "exalted one". Long is the day and long is the night, and long is my waiting. I have sometimes appeared as The Fisher King.'

That night I racked my brains for his name. Tomorrow would be my last opportunity to guess. I listed all the things which we had collected . There were: three mermaids' hairs; a key; a box; a ring; a feather; a chess piece; a candlestick; a rope; a toy car; a ship in a bottle; a basket; and a shell.

All the characters and motifs in the stories, the women, men, animals, fairies, creatures, powerful forces from the underworld became quite muddled in my head. None seem to point to his name, even though he had given me some clues.

I decided to bake some bread. It always helps me to think, and besides, I could take him a loaf for his journey as a parting gift. He had evidently eaten all of the last bake and perhaps bread was a missing token. The thought struck me that we now had twelve tokens and as a storyteller I thought that thirteen, a baker's dozen, was more appropriate.

I realised as I kneaded the dough that I was really going to miss him, even though he was often grumpy, ill-mannered, angry, impossible. I had grown fond of him and had enjoyed our missions, and the journey. I had learnt a lot and he had helped in assembling an unusual selection of stories.

I left the dough to prove overnight. I would bake it early in the morning so that it would still be hot when I handed it to him. I fell asleep quite easily, but had some very strange dreams, a jumble of all the objects I had listed, a whirl of sights and sounds and colours, fragments of this and that from the last few weeks.

When I woke up next morning, the bed was a mess. The covers were on the floor and the pillows had taken up a new place at the foot of the bed. I got up and found my partner sitting in his dressing gown. He told me he had to get up because I was thrashing about so much it made sleep impossible for him. He said I was talking in my sleep. I quickly asked what I had said, thinking it may point the way to a name. On his notebook he had written: 'An arrow straight and true.' I frowned. It didn't seem to make a name. I kneaded the bread again.

Suddenly it came to me. I kept it to myself, needing to roll the thoughts around in my head, whilst kneading and rolling the bread dough. After baking the bread I wrapped two small loaves in a clean cloth, put them in my rucksack and set off.

# CWM CYCH

We were to meet at the crossroads in Cwm Cych. I told him about nearby Clynfyw, where a family farm grew organic food. They had commissioned local artists to create a sculpture trail and a roundhouse. My companion said he knew about that and had given them some inspiration.

From the crossroads we walked along a lane which had two possible entries to the Otherworld. The trees along this lane made a magnificent avenue, standing like sentinels almost as if they were showing the way. The first place we came to had all the expected characteristics. It was shaped like a bowl cut out of the rock face at the side of the road. The water from dripping springs seeped out of the rock, but it was difficult to see anything clearly because it was so overgrown.

I had brought some garden secateurs and cut away some of the bramble, bindweed and ivy to see if we could find the entrance. My friend was frowning, looking up at the sky. I guessed that he was worried about the time. Eventually he shook his head. 'It's not right.'

He wanted to walk further along the lane. I was now worried about the time, even though I had no idea what was to happen and when. But he was insistent, so we walked another mile or so. We came to a similar place, again shaped like a bowl cut from the rock at the side of the road. This place had less undergrowth. My companion spied a small tree growing at one side and nodded. He proclaimed that this was the place.

I helped him to search for the entrance. We found a fissure in the rock, covered with lichen and moss, very damp. We scraped away some of the growth and found some markings carved in the stone. He smiled, then turned, held my hand and thanked me. It made me glow; his thanks were very special since they were not easily bestowed.

'Wait!' I said, and reached in my rucksack for the bread. I handed him the cloth parcel. He placed the loaves on the top of the basket already full with objects for his journey. He said that he must be alone to get through the first doorway. I placed a kiss on his cheek. He blushed and looked very embarrassed, but smiled. He gave me a gift. It was a smooth stone with a red hue, very beautiful. I thanked him and said I would always treasure it. I would place it on my workbench, where it would be a constant reminder of our adventures and an inspiration for more stories.

He told me to be careful not to rub it too hard for too long, because that would be a cry for help. It would summon him to help me if I needed it, and he would not be best pleased to make this journey again just because I had been careless in handling the stone. I promised to handle it with care. I started to walk away so that he could be alone, then I suddenly remembered about guessing his name. 'Wait,' I shouted and I ran to where he was and whispered in his ear. He smiled and thanked me again.

'This means a special magic will accompany my journey and protect me.' I had no idea what this meant but I knew enough not to question him.

I smiled and walked away. When I reached the road, I turned to wave, but he had gone.

I arrived home and felt very flat. Would I ever see him again? Would I ever be privileged again to hear his magical stories? The little man had dominated my life for more than a fortnight and I was already missing him.

I remembered something that I always say to a storytelling audience about sharing the tales that they have heard. It was now my duty to share all of these stories, to keep them alive in the way that storytellers have done for centuries. I sat in my studio and wrote and wrote and wrote into the night. This book is the result. I hope you like it.

## Now it's your turn

See if you can guess my companion's name. Please email your guess to christinestories@yahoo.co.uk by Hen Galan (12 January 2014).

On this day, the first person to have correctly guessed the name of my companion on this journey through *Pembrokeshire Folk Tales* will win three titles of their choice in this series of folk tales.

## The story of Culhwch and Olwen

If your are wondering if I ever heard the story of Culhwch and Olwen, which my companion cut short in the Nevern churchyard, go to the publisher's website (www.thehistorypress.co.uk) and you can read it for yourself, and hear me reading it.

Two days after my farewell to my friend, I found a small parcel in the window box beside my front door, wrapped in the cloth that had contained the bread. It was the key. The next day I made my way to Pentre Ifan. I knocked on the door of Sioned's house. The door was, as ever, ajar but there was no answer to my knock. I went into the garden and replaced the key in the lock. As I passed the open door again a voice called out 'Diolch' (thanks).

A week or so later I found the chess piece on the gatepost as I was leaving my house to meet with a representative from an organisation which looked after ancient monuments. They were looking for a storyteller to do some work for them. I put the chessman in my pocket for luck, then put it back in the shirt collar box when I returned home.

Several weeks after that, my mother's ring was returned. I was weeding the kitchen garden when I saw it on the stem of a leek. I had planted a whole bed of leeks just before my adventure had begun.

A month later the wooden box appeared on the front doorstep. I placed it by the cromlech at Pentre Ifan since I guessed that's where it had come from.

During the course of the following year many of the objects were returned. It became a bit of a game to find them, and to guess what would be next. I was pleased because these are the objects that I take in the basket to story workshops. You might also like to get a basket which you could start to fill with objects that tell stories too.

I am still waiting for my mother's handkerchief.

# BIBLIOGRAPHY & FURTHER READING

## BOOKS

Cope, P., *Holy Wells: Wales – A Photographic Journey* (Seren, 2008)

Davies, M., *Save the Last of the Magic* (E.L. Jones & Son, 1993)

Mason, R., *Tales and Traditions of Tenby* (Tenby Museum Archives, 1858)

Medlicott, M., *Shemi's Tall Tales* (Pont Books, 2008)

Evans-Wentz, W.Y., *The Fairy Faith in Celtic Countries* (1911)

Yorke, P., *William Haggar: Fairground Film Maker* (Accent Press Ltd, 2007)

Guest, Lady Charlotte, trans., *The Mabinogion* (J.M. Dent, 1906)

Davies, Sioned, *The Mabinogion* (Oxford University Press, 2008)

## OTHER

Bertram Lloyd 1881–1944, unpublished writings (Tenby Museum Archives)

Drayton, M., *Poly-Olbion*

Southey, R., *The poetical works of Robert Southey: Madoc in Wales*

Williams, W., *The Peacemakers*, translated by Tony Conran (Gomer Press) – *see* Tony Conran's new poem about Pentre Ifan, Portal Dolmen in Pembrokeshire dedicated to the memory of Peter Llewelyn, Poetry Wales, January 2013.

If you enjoyed this book, you may also be interested in…

## Denbighshire Folk Tales

FIONA COLLINS

Wales is especially rich in folklore, and
Fiona Collins has collected a wide range
of tales here. While many of them will
be familiar to Welsh speakers, people
unfamiliar with the culture and customs
of the county will find some fascinating
and unusual tales. As one of the oldest
inhabited area of Wales, the varied
landscape of Denbighshire has inspired
stories of magic, dragons and devils, and
ordinary people doing extraordinary
things.

978 0 7524 5187 9

## Gloucestershire Folk Tales

ANTHONY NANSON

Gloucestershire's history is rich with
myth and magic. The landscapes of the
county, from the rolling Cotswolds to the
Forest of Dean, the bustling metropolis
of Gloucester to the ancient Berkeley
Castle, are steeped in stories. These tales
will introduce you to lonely ghosts, fairies,
and wild beasts roaming the woodlands.
The intriguing stories collected here are
brought vividly to life by a passionate and
knowledgeable local storyteller.

978 0 7524 6017 8

Visit our website and discover thousands of
other History Press books.

**www.thehistorypress.co.uk**